Taming the Little Devils Within

Author
Dr. Amit Abraham

UNICORN BOOKS

Publisher
UNICORN BOOKS
F-2/16, Ansari Road, Daryaganj, New Delhi-110002
☎ 23275434, 23262683, 23262783 • Fax: 011-23257790
E-mail: info@unicornbooks.in • *Website:* www.unicornbooks.in

Distributor
Pustak Mahal®
J-3/16, Daryaganj, New Delhi-110002
☎ 23276539, 23272783, 23272784 • Fax: 011-23260518
E-mail: info@pustakmahal.com • *Website:* www.pustakmahal.com

Sales Centres
- **Delhi:**
  - 10-B, Netaji Subhash Marg, Daryaganj, New Delhi-110002
    ☎ 23268292, 23268293, 23279900 • Fax: 011-23280567
    E-mail: salespmahal@airtelmail.in, rapidexdelhi@indiatimes.com
  - 6686, Khari Baoli, Delhi-110006
    ☎ 23944314, 23911979
- **Bengaluru:** ☎ 080-22234025 • Telefax: 080-22240209
  E-mail: pustak@airtelmail.in • pustak@sancharnet.in
- **Mumbai:** ☎ 022-22010941, 022-22053387
  E-mail: rapidex@bom5.vsnl.net.in
- **Patna:** ☎ 0612-3294193 • Telefax: 0612-2302719
  E-mail: rapidexptn@rediffmail.com
- **Hyderabad:** Telefax: 040-24737290
  E-mail: pustakmahalhyd@yahoo.co.in

ISBN: 978-81-7806-211-2

Edition: September 2010

Printed at : Param Offsetters, Okhla, New Delhi-110020

This book is dedicated
to
the mentally challenged
who
truly understand the language of love
in this otherwise sane world.

Acknowledgement

This book was a Herculean task, which would not have been possible without the cooperation and support of those people whom I wish to thank from the very bottom of my heart.

First and foremost I wish to thank the publishers for the patience they showed giving me ample of time to finish writing this book. After having given me this proposal, they had to wait for two long years for the work to finish. I hope and pray that this patience of theirs is rewarding.

I would like to thank my friends who constantly kept motivating and encouraging me to keep going ahead with the writing work despite various obstacles that came in the way.

Thanks are also due to friends of Samvaidna: The Mental Health Organization who have grouped together in order to address the psychological problems of the readers on Face Book

Above all, I wish to acknowledge the support of my wife and daughter throughout the writing of this book and without which the writing of this book would never have finished.

–Dr. Amit Abraham

"Knowing your own darkness is the best method for dealing with the darknesss' of other people.

Your vision will become clear only when you can look into your own heart. Who looks outside, dreams; who looks inside, awakes"

-Carl Jung

Contents

Introduction

Me And The Devils - A Case Study

"We are each our own devil, and we make this world our hell".

I have written many books on psychology, both text and self-help ones, but writing this book has given me an altogether new experience – a deeper insight into the common psychological problems experienced by a majority of the population. Though I have been teaching psychology since the last two decades and involved with research and measurement work, this experience enriched my understanding of abnormal psychology as well. I realized that though we are the masters of our mental health but we create and then submit ourselves as slaves to the conditions, which make us mentally unhealthy. I wish to elaborate on this issue and share a case, which I handled some years back. Looking back, I find it as a perfect example of how a mentally healthy individual can invite, create, and aggravate conditions, which adversely affect his psychological wellbeing. This case study will help you relate and understand things better as you browse through this book. The words marked in *italics* have technical meanings related with mental health. You will find them explained in detail further on in the book. The name of the 'client' has also been changed for protecting his identity.

THE BIRTH OF THE LITTLE DEVILS

Arpit was a freelance journalist trying hard to make his place in the competitive fourth estate – the world of the press. What was frustrating for him was that circumstances had forced him to give up a job as a subeditor in a prestigious local newspaper. Thereafter, he had applied at various other places but *discrimination* got the better of him. He was still fortunate to have a fat bank balance and a well-furnished apartment, both by virtue of inheritance from his late parents. In the apartment the only things which actually belonged to him was a computer placed on a specially designed computer-cum-study table and a laptop, which he had purchased a few years back.

Arpit spent most of the time sitting on his computer table writing articles and translating books for small-time publishers. This was not his source of bread and butter but a means and mode of satisfying his creative *urges*. He eagerly looked forward each day with hope for a better tomorrow. However, that tomorrow was not coming and *frustration* getting the better of him. On top of this, his elder sister sent her twelve-years-old daughter to stay with him and study in the metropolitan city for a better education.

No sooner had his niece arrived to stay with Arpit, he got a lucrative offer from a very big publisher for writing a general interest book but with the condition that it should be finished within three months. Arpit signed the agreement seeing it as a launching pad into the creative writing profession. However, little did he realize what was there in store for him. He had planned things according to the present set of circumstances and hoped to achieve his *goal* in the coming future. However, this was not to be so. Things did not go the way as he had planned, and in trying to resolve his problems, he adopted desperate measures thus aggravating them even more.

The present set of circumstances forced him to become a single parent to his niece. All the time he had in the world suddenly seemed to shrink into minutes and seconds. His daily schedule got disturbed and he had to reschedule the same. Getting up at five in the morning was never his habit and working late in the night his style. He was not only forced to get up early but also sleep early as well. The early morning hours of his were spent doing odd household chores. The time he got when his niece was in school was utilized visiting the various offices of newspaper, magazines and publication houses looking for a job or submitting articles for publication consideration. This changed daily routine, and additional responsibilities of home management brought about *adjustment problems* for both him and his niece. He was so accustomed to absolute independence and his niece had been so very dependent for everything on her mother. It is very difficult for him to fill in the shoes of her mother and he found himself failing on all counts inviting *stress* and *anxieties* in addition to the frustration he already had.

Apart from the changed daily routine his personal space also shrunk. His studious niece who would spend most of the time studying seized his specially designed computer-cum-study table. He simply had no access to the computer for doing his writing work or browsing the internet at leisure for information and knowledge. He was in no mood to buy another study table and chair, which would unnecessarily fill up the empty space in his house. Honestly, as he admitted, he had a little *claustrophobia*. His apartment was not filled up with unnecessary things and there was a lot of space to move around freely. In fact, he joked about taking his morning walk inside the apartment.

Another problem, which cropped up was his stubborn habit of keeping things in a highly organized manner. He was a *perfectionist* by its definition and his niece a highly unorganized person. She was no match to his standards of perfection. This disorganization became a regular issue of argument between them.

FAMILY HISTORY

Arpit's parents were both doctors employed in a government hospital. He had a sister who was ten years elder to him. Aprit was admitted into a boarding school at the age of six and studied there until his twelfth standard. When thereafter he came to stay with his parents to do his graduation both his parents died in a tragic road accident. His sister who had been married to a businessman and settled in a small city took up the responsibility of his education and upbringing. Arpit completed his graduation and thereafter did a diploma in journalism and mass communication. Soon after finishing the diploma, he found employment in a local newspaper as a press reporter in the city where his ancestral home was. His sister and brother-in-law had been honest and gracious enough to pass down all the money and properties that belonged to the parents.

THE LITTLE DEVILS

The new set of situations and circumstances in which Arpit found himself very soon began to show their effect upon him. His upbringing was tinted with the negativity of *institutionalization* which had made him into an individual who lacked emotional warmth, was attention seeking, overly dramatic, self-centered, shallow in relationship, had difficulty in interpersonal relationships, had a low tolerance for delayed gratification, and unable to cope with stress. He wanted everything well organized, to follow fixed schedules, and had a rigid attitude towards life and things. In short, he had a *histrionic personality* with shades of *obsessive-compulsive personality*. With his past psychological makeup and the present set of circumstances, Arpit found himself harbouring and nourishing the little devils within him. He began loosing his mental balance and exhibit symptoms, which are associated with many common psychological problems. At times, he also wondered he had gone crazy. Let me first share with you the various psychological problems I encountered while giving counselling to Arpit. This sharing of my experience in this case should enrich you with realistic inputs and when reading the book you can further associate them well.

Adjustment Problems: The first psychological problems Arpit encountered were adjustments. His daily routine was disturbed. He had either to adapt his routine to the new set of circumstances or try striking a balance. This appeared as an impossible task to him as he did not want to change. His freedom to do things as per his wish was now captivated because of the new role he had to play in child rearing. His personal space was also encroached. He needed to work for long periods in solitude on the computer, which now was not possible. All these things coupled with his upbringing, unemployment and a few others appeared like huge obstacles in his *goal-directed behaviour*. His creative urges began to be thwarted resulting in additional *frustration*. This added more fuel to the fire, which was already burning in his life. In short, he was finding it difficult to handle the various *adjustive demands*.

Stress: He very soon began to feel stress upon himself because of the readjust he was being forced to make in his daily routine activities. He had been used to a fixed schedule. Every activity of his had its specific time but now the only fixed schedule was getting up at five in the morning and sleeping early in the night. This type of unstable schedule acted as a stressor upon him and he began to feel the mounting discomfort.

Mental Fatigue: He found himself surrounded by problems and was unable to tackle them. The failure to do tensed him. This tension began to reflect upon him and he began feeling exhausted doing even the daily household chores. He experienced pain in his muscles and joints as well as a decline in energy levels. This was accompanied by a decrease in his concentration power. All these indicated that he was getting mentally fatigued.

Anxiety: He began feeling inadequate in handling the new situation, which soon began to appear threatening to him. He felt that his *achievement drive* and need for *self-actualization* have met a dead end. He would no longer be able to pursue his writing works and get a decent job. He soon began feeling insecure from not only being unemployed but also being employable. He feared of being reduced to nothing more than a domestic help. All these thoughts coupled made him feel anxious. His anxiety was also reflected in his having *panic attacks* sometimes.

Depression: His feelings of depression were due to a combination of various factors – suppressed anger, stress, and perfectionist nature. He cut himself off from the world around and remained glued to the television most of the time he was free at home. Hobbies and things, which in the past appealed to him, now disinterested him. He became quite forgetful and got irritated easily.

Phobia: His little claustrophobia was not letting him do adjustments and make alternative arrangements for his working setup. He simply was not bowing down to the demand of buying an additional study table and chair for his niece. He wanted empty space in his apartment even if it was emptying all the happiness out of his life. Phobias sometimes can really drive you crazy by their side effects.

Sleep Disorders: Early to bed and early to rise was surely not making him healthy and wise. The stress, coupled with anxiety and depression, was disturbing his sleep. The routine of his sleep had also changed suddenly and he was not getting adequate sleep. Many times, he took a nap in the noontime but then going to sleep in the night was like a nightmare for him. Without proper sleep, he just felt lifeless throughout the day.

Irritable Mood: His frustrations were making him react in an irritated manner towards things and people. The mood of his was spoiling relationships with family and friends. He began to show verbal aggression on the road while driving, or with people, he casually interacted. At large, sister, brother-in-law, and niece had to bear most of the brunt of his irritated mood, which began to disturb the peace in the small family.

Forgetfulness: He wished hard how he could forget all about the past and go into a state of *retrograde amnesia* unable to recall painful memories, which have caused him immense pain. The perfectionist that he was he did suffer from mild forgetting especially related with the task he was compelling himself to do. The little writing he would manage to do was beıng jumbled up because he could not remember and relate to what he had written in the previous session. His mental fatigue and depressive state were also effecting his memory and creating forgetfulness. However, experiences, bad or good, are there for sharing and learning.

Obsessive-Compulsive Behaviour: Arpit got into a habit of constantly thinking about tasks, which he had accomplished long back, he would lie down in bed and count the edges of the wirings repeatedly. When he left the house, he wondered if all was well back there. These were showing his obsessed thoughts. His compulsive behaviours related with excessive double-checking of things, such as locks, appliances, and switches. Repeatedly calling up his sister on the phone and checking to see if she was fine and adjusting things to keep them back in the right position. He also used to get troubled if he could not complete an unnecessary act. Some of his obsessive thoughts and compulsive acts were there since the past few years they were presently being used by him to wade of his high level of anxiety.

THE TAMING

By now, you must have begun to wonder how a single individual can suffer from so many psychological problems at one time and that too over such a small issue. The answer is that the onset of any psychological problem does not only have a present but also a past and future. Many of the problems are related and interdependent with overlapping symptoms. Its severity depends on ones susceptibility, and the degree to which the symptoms are exhibited. Arpit was perfectly normal but highly susceptible. This was because of his personality makeup, which was largely groomed by his upbringing. Some advice from my end and a greater effort on his part helped him overcome the problem. How he managed it, I will surely share with you.

Arpit began to frequently visit me in my clinic and share his problems. I began advising him to make minor adjustments and slowly accept the change in the circumstances. However, psychological advice is not like a pharmaceutical drug, which, if taken as advised, cures you in a magical manner. It took him a good four to five months to resolve his problems and make the necessary adjustments and changes. How he did it, I will surely share with you. Remember if you have to free yourself from a psychological problem you have to follow the advice on a regular basis and it will only begin to show positive results when the advice you are following becomes a habit for you. A habit because you have to live following the advice or else there will be a relapse. You have to tame yourself accordingly.

In an effort to tame the little devils within him, Arpit first tried what almost everyone does. Force others to adapt themselves according to our way of things. He asked his niece to find another comfortable place in the house for her studies – the beds, the dining table or the sofa in the drawing room. She was very adjusting and for a few days kept shifting her spot for her studies from one room to the other. However, she did not feel comfortable in any location and demanded that he purchase for her a separate study table and a revolving chair with wheels. Arpit simply did not give in to her demands because of the empty space he required in the house. This relentless on his part infuriated things and his sister showed her annoyance over the phone. She reminded him of all the sacrifices she had made in bringing him up after the death of the parents and now it was his turn to do something for her. There was a lot of arguments but ultimately the maternal uncle in him made the sacrifice and gave over the special table and chair.

Having surrendered the table and chair, he could not do his writing work, which brought in symptoms associated with the various psychological problems I have mentioned. Time passed and his problems seemed to worsen. He soon realized that the advice I was giving to him might prove useful. He got down thinking about the adjustments suggested by me and coped with the situation with realistic thinking. The first thing he did was to take out his laptop, which he had not been using since the last many months. To his agony, he discovered its battery was dead. However, he plugged it into the power socket and began with his writing works. The long power cuts became another source of irritation for him as they mostly occurred during the period he was a bit free. He decided to purchase a new battery for the laptop. It was not available with the company, as the model had been phased out. He was back to square one. The performance of his laptop was also not good because of less random access memory. He was told in a shop that the same could not be enhanced. He did not give up the search and finally found a compatible battery and the random access memory chip. He also connected the computers via wireless and enabled file sharing. Now his machine was well-equipped and sitting on the bed, he began with the writing work.

The bed is not a comfortable place for sitting and typing on the laptop for long periods. He began to have pain in the neck, back and the knee joints. Moreover, he was unable to concentrate because of the various other daily tasks he had to do or were pending asking for his immediate attention. His disturbed and inadequate sleep was making him feel drowsy. It was then that he decided that he would have to make more adjustments. The nap in the day was cancelled. He designed and ordered a table, just small enough to keep the notebook, along with a small chair. This saved space and provided a comfortable sitting posture – claustrophobia managed.

With time, he managed to tune his routine and accommodate everything – work, home, shopping and even outings. The intermittent disturbances became a part of his concentration and he stopped bothering about them. He also realized that though every moment was precious for him but moments of peace, calm and tranquility missed out are invaluable. Without a good mental health, his existence would be just like a brief crack of light between two eternities of darkness.

This case is some six or seven years old and today Arpit is a famous mass media personality, a host of many a talk shows and an author of some bestselling books. He may have forgotten me but I do remember his case because it has inspired me to write this book. I look forward to your taking help from this case and relating what you read in this book with the same. It will help you practically understand things in a better manner and benefit. I wish you and your family a good mental health.

I request you to kindly e-mail to me your comments on the statements of the tests and scales you find in this book as judged by you in terms of their relevance and ambiguity. Also kindly send me the scores you obtain on the various measures given in the book especially your scores on the Defense Mechanism Scale – for each subtest, along with information about your age, sex, education, and nationality. Your scores will enable me to validate the measures.

Chapter 1

The Normalcy Hype

"I have gradually come to one negative conclusion about the good life. It seems to me that the good life is not any fixed state. It is not, in my estimation, a state of virtue, or contentment, or nirvana, or happiness. It is not a condition in which, the individual is adjusted, or fulfilled, or actualized. To use psychological terms, it is not a state of drive- reduction, or tension - reduction or homeostasis. The good life is a process, not a state of being. It is a direction not a destination."

—Carl Rogers

"A sharp dividing line between normal and abnormal behaviour simply does not exist"

With the advent of science and technology, humankind has been able to conquer over many of the physical ills, which had afflicted them for the past many centuries. Over these centuries humankind has been enlightened, endowed with reason, and progressed, but not without paying a price for all these accomplishments. Today the fortunate majority is no longer a victim of famines and epidemics. The black plague though has been overpowered and eradicated but it seems to have been replaced with a host of psychological plagues. These look subtle but are extremely lethal, spreading within like a cancer, taking their toll slowly but surely. There is worry, value conflicts, loneliness, disillusionment, and doubts. We are too engrossed chasing our dreams, blindly running through mazes and dark blind alleys or have lost our way in there. The lucky ones who have managed to find their way through seem not too contended with what they have ultimately achieved. This is what the mirage of modern existence is. In the end, all are equally besieged with the pangs of anxiety. No wonder this age is aptly called the *Age of Anxiety*.

Normalcy today has nearly become a myth. Mostly all of us are beset with seemingly endless personal and social problems. There have been wars, social unrest, economic recession, unemployment, personal grief, and many such psychosocial and economical problems, which have disrupted our life directly or indirectly affecting our mental wellbeing. Darwin's law of survival of the fittest has moved from the jungle into the civilized population. There is constant pressure to succeed on the young child, escalating with each target he achieves. The steps on the ladder are infinite and no end for the human desires to satiate. The fulfilled desires soon become meaningless and newer unfulfilled ones constantly aggravate man's anxieties.

Look around you and you will find on every side anxious, unhappy, bewildered people who are missing the fulfillment of their best potential because they cannot achieve a satisfactory adjustment to problems that seem just too great. Smooth, effective functioning has been eclipsed by symptoms of personality maladjustment. In many cases, the stress of modern life takes its toll leading to psychiatric causality. The statistics show that mental illness incapacitates more people than all other health problems combined. It may be a bitter fact but all of us, to some extent, show some or the other characteristics that deviates us from the normalcy mark. The abnormal behaviour of ours may though be just a matter of degrees but the question does arise on "How normal are we"?

The layman may not agree with what is being claimed here but abnormal behaviour is not only the extreme, bizarre, and sensational things that we see in mental hospitals and clinics. It also includes anxiety, depression, phobias, and moods, sleep disturbances, obsessive or compulsive behaviour and many others. We all suffer from one or the other psychological problems during our life span yet claiming ourselves to be normal and mentally healthy individuals. It is lack of awareness, which makes things miserable for us. It is time that we wake up to this bitter reality and put in our conscious efforts for living a better mentally healthy and adjusted life.

While going through this book you need not be besieged by fears feeling that you are a deviant from the normal. Many people occasionally feel anxious, discouraged, and inadequate for days and months together. Their behaviour is irrational, irritable and restless. They feel unduly fatigued, experience loss of appetite and have sleep disturbances. This however, does not always indicate that they are neurotic. These symptoms can be the resultant of psychological stresses, which impinge upon such individuals due to various reasons. Almost everyone experiences feelings of insecurity and anxiety resulting from various life situations so your exhibited symptoms just make you a part of the larger world of normally deviant individuals.

However, I would like to sound caution along with making you a part of the normally deviant individuals. Though most of us are minor deviants from normalcy, some may have crossed over the danger mark. This requires psychiatric and psychological intervention for diagnosis and treatment. It should not be treated lightly since delay will only cause harm. While going through this book and doing evaluations if you feel that you are one of them then remember that mental illness is not a disgrace. Do not be reluctant to get professional help at the earliest. Your positive acceptance will enable you to recover, saving the elevation of difficulties in the end. Your treatment is for the betterment for your own wellbeing and that of your family.

Chapter: 2

Dimensions of Mental Health

"It is often tragic to see how blatantly a man bungles his own life and the lives of others yet remain totally incapable of seeing how much the whole tragedy originates in himself, and how he continually feeds it and keeps it going". Carl Gustav Jung

"Everything that irritates us about others can lead us to an understanding about ourselves."

In order to diagnose, treat, and eventually prevent abnormal behaviour, we must start by knowing about the basics of mental health. Many times, we are irritated by the behaviour of other people and label them as abnormal. The reverse of the same is also applicable – we irritate other people with our behaviour. In both these cases, a seemingly normal behaviour appears abnormal to the beholder. All behaviours done reflect directly upon our mental health which from time to time is influenced by situations and circumstances. One is rarely ever in a state of absolute equilibrium. We keep deviating from norms, which govern and define normal behaviour. However, with a few exceptions, there are some clearly defined norms and specific criterions laid down, which define our mental health on a relatively permanent basis. To evaluate and understand our behaviour and that of others we need to know about these distinct dimensions of mental health.

SOME DISTINCT DIMENSIONS OF MENTAL HEALTH

One of the most important things required for people to develop into healthy individuals is having a good mental health. Our personality cannot function normally if we do not have a sound mental health. People lacking good mental health exhibit symptoms of personality maladjustment. This can be attributed to lacking either one or many characteristics, which constitute ones normal psychological functioning. On the other hand, good mental health is indicated by a psychological state of well-being, characterized by continuing personal growth, a sense of purpose in life, self-acceptance, and positive relations with others.

Psychologists have identified many distinct dimensions of mental health. These include: *self-acceptance*, or *self-esteem*, characterized by a positive evaluation of oneself and one's past experiences; personal growth reflected in one's sense of continued psychological growth and development; a sense that one's life has purpose and meaning; positive relations with others; environmental mastery, the capacity to manage effectively in the surrounding world; and autonomy, a sense of self-determination and the ability to control one's own life. Self-acceptance, relations with others, environmental mastery, and autonomy usually improve as a person ages and gains life experience. However, many people find that their personal growth and sense of purpose in life begin to decline in midlife.

Some psychologists regard mental health as the ability to maintain a balance between positive and negative emotions, such as elation and sadness. In this view, a person who displays emotional extremes in either direction is less well adjusted. Other psychologists emphasize the role of one's environment in influencing well-being. This perspective sees mental health reflected in a person's overall happiness with various domains of life, such as social relationships, work, and community life.

FACTORS INFLUENCING MENTAL HEALTH

A number of different aspects of life can influence mental health. These areas are working life, family life, and the social role that one occupies in the community. Negative experiences in these areas, such as an unreasonable boss or a turbulent family life, can reduce one's overall sense of well-being.

Another important influence on mental health is *stress*. In general, people experience stress when the demands placed on them exceed the resources they have available to meet those demands. Significant sources of stress include major life events, such as divorce, death of a spouse, loss of a job, and illness in the family. These events can overwhelm a person's ability to cope and function effectively. In addition, one source of stress may lead to another, as when financial hardship follows job loss. People who experience unusually traumatic events, such as rape and natural disasters, may develop post-traumatic stress disorder.

People may experience chronic stress when confronted with a continuing set of demands that reduce their ability to function. Examples of such demands include working long hours under difficult circumstances and caring for a chronically ill relative. Economic hardship, unemployment, and poverty can also produce chronic stress and undermine mental health.

Some studies suggest that genetic factors may partly determine one's level of happiness and mental health. People seem to display a characteristic level of well-being, with some people usually feeling happy and others typically feeling sad or unhappy. Researchers have found that although people's moods change in response to both positive and negative events, the effect wears off over time. For example, people who win the lottery or receive an unexpected promotion may feel happier at first, but over time, they return to their former characteristic level of mental health. Research suggests that one's genetic background—that is, the genes inherited from one's parents—explains more than half of the differences in people's characteristic mood levels. Genes may also partly determine the range of difficulties that people feel, including whether people have large mood swings or remain stable from day to day.

EVALUATE YOUR MENTAL HEALTH

This scale is constructed by me based upon the various characteristics, which determine the mental health of an individual. You are requested to respond to each statement in accordance with your true feelings. The test is in two parts. Read each statement carefully and then assign the "point" (0-3) in the blank space provided at the beginning of each statement. *The point you choose to assign is to be based on the frequency of occurrences with regard to the given statement.* ***The points are different for both the parts and are mentioned in the beginning***. Be honest because honesty with self in one of the significant characteristics of a mentally healthy individual. Kindly note this is not a standardized scale, but only a rough measure of your mental health and not meant for medical or legal purposes.

PART I

Points For Part I

0 – Never.

1 – Sometimes.

2 – Most of the time.

3 – Always.

______ 1. I have the freedom to take my own decisions.
______ 2. I can do all my things independently.
______ 3. I know the directions I have to take for doing my tasks.
______ 4. I am confident about my abilities while doing a job.
______ 5. I have the ability to take on responsibility.
______ 6. I put in needed efforts to achieve my goals.
______ 7. Other people rely on me.
______ 8. I am persistent in all that I do.
______ 9. I find time to devote for my hobbies.
______ 10. The opposite sex finds me attractive.
______ 11. I get along well with my superiors.
______ 12. I follow rules and regulations.
______ 13. I like healthy competition.
______ 14. I am satisfied with everything in life.
______ 15. I feel secure.
______ 16. I like making friends.
______ 17. I express my love freely.
______ 18. I like giving gifts to others.
______ 19. I like receiving gifts from others.
______ 20. I am very tolerant towards the irrational behaviours of others.
______ 21. I handle my frustrations well.
______ 22. I am in control of my emotions.
______ 23. I contribute in cash/kind towards social causes.
______ 24. I watch lighthearted shows on television.
______ 25. I put service before self.
______ 26. I share intimate (not sexual but close) relations with my friends/colleagues.

______ 27. I cooperate with others members in my group/office while doing tasks assigned.

______ 28. I cooperate with my spouse/ parents at home.

______ 29. I look at everything in life in a positive manner.

______ 30. I ask help from others when required.

______ **Total For Part 1**.

PART II

Points For Part II

0 - Always.

1 – Most of the time.

2 – Sometimes.

3 - Never.

______ 1. I am not confident about my abilities.

______ 2. Small problems easily upset me.

______ 3. I am worried about my future.

______ 4. I lack the ability to take decisions.

______ 5. I have mood fluctuations.

______ 6. I suffer from feelings of insecurity.

______ 7. Others have to help me make decisions.

______ 8. Even when in a group I do not feel secure.

______ 9. I feel that I am loosing self-respect.

______ 10. I cannot decide for final even when I want to do a particular thing.

______ 11. I have a feeling that some calamities will occur with me.

______ 12. I cannot finish tasks in one go.

______ 13. I am unable to solve my problems myself.

______ 14. I feel that my future is not well planned and defined.

______ 15. I shirk away from responsibilities.

______ 16. I am not able to take quick decisions on any matter.

______ 17. I feel that this world is very hostile.

______ 18. I need a conducive work environment.

______ 19. I am unsatisfied with my life's cutput.

______ 20. I become hopeless when I fail in any task.

______ 21. I do not get along well with the people in the locality my house is in.

______ 22. I feel depressed and dejected.

______ 23. I suffer from feelings of inferiority.

______ 24. I am enraged even by the slightest unfavorable talk.

______ 25. I feel my life is a burden for others in my family.

______ 26. Minor difficulties disappoint me.

______ 27. I lack concentration while working.

______ 28. I build castles in the air.

______ 29. I do not have a flexible approach.

______ 30. In adverse circumstances, I act without keeping real facts in view.]

______ **Total For Part 2.**

SCORING AND INTERPRETATION

After you have assigned the points for both the parts total them up. Add up the total score of part 1 and part 2 and you will get your total mental health score. If your score lies in the range of 136 – 180 you have an *extremely good mental health*; in the range of 91 - 135, your mental health is *good;* in the range of 46 – 90, you have *average mental health;* and if it is in the range of 0 – 45 you have *poor mental health* and you need to identify upon your weak area and act accordingly to improve upon the same. Further chapters in this book will help you identify you weak mental health areas and guide you accordingly.

Chapter 3

Origin of the Little Devils – Causes of Abnormal Behaviour

"The type of adjustment that an individual is achieving at any time is a function of both his psychobiological development and the stress situation confronting him. Anything, which led to faulty development or that which increases stress, may bring trouble. In some cases it is the stress which plays the dominant role whereas in others faulty personality development seems chiefly responsible for the abnormal behaviour. However, in most cases both development and stress factors play important roles. There are also disorders, which are primarily sociogenic in nature - in which sociological factors induce distortions in development or create stresses, which are not too great for healthy development. Whichever factor out of the three plays a dominant role they have their major contributions in the development of abnormal behaviour".

"People's behaviour makes sense if you think about it in terms of their goals, needs, and motives"

Psychology deals with how we think, feel, and act as we face different situations each day. It is about how we look at our lives, the people in our lives, and ourselves. It also includes how we handle stress, how we relate to others, and how we go about making our decisions All these and many more reflect upon our total personality makeup. This make up in turn is dependent upon and affected by various factors, which play a crucial role in our mental health. If someone has a poor mental health, his various psychological processes will not work appropriately and cause pain and agony. He will not be able to perform simple tasks, maintain healthy relationships with family and friends, and his professional life will be hampered. There is a seemingly endless list of maladaptive behaviours, which a mentally unhealthy individual can exhibit. The question is what and who is responsible for this unhealthy development of the individual. There is no one answer as the range of factors responsible varies from biological factors such as genetics, chemical imbalances, or damage to the central nervous system to a combination of these factors with psychosocial and socio-cultural ones. We will discuss each one of these separately relating them with the other.

BIOLOGICAL FACTORS

Chemical Imbalance: Researches have shown that some mental illnesses are linked to an abnormal balance of special chemicals in the brain called *neurotransmitters*. The function of these neurotransmitters is to help the nerve cells in the brain to effectively communicate with each other. If a chemical imbalance occurs or they malfunction then a communication failure can happen within the brain itself, leading to exhibition of such symptoms which are considered abnormal.

Injuries And Defects: Apart from these chemical imbalances, injuries caused to specific areas of the brain can also result in its malfunctioning. This in turn leads to behaviours, which are considered abnormal. In the same manner, defects in specific areas of the brain can become causes of abnormal behaviours. These defects may be since birth or due to some injury or serious illness or disease.

Genetics (Heredity): It has been observed through the study of family case histories that many mental illnesses run in the family. These observations suggest a genetic link to specific mental illnesses. Findings suggest that these mental illnesses are the resultant of abnormalities in the structure of the genes. Thus, there is a high probability that parents suffering from some mental illness may transmit the same genetically to their offspring's. However, there are times that though a person may inherit a susceptibility to a mental illness but does not necessarily develop the same. This is because some mental illnesses along with being linked to the genes are also largely dependent on environmental factor such as stress, abuse, or a traumatic event. These environmental factors can influence or trigger an illness in a person who is inherently susceptible to it.

Infections: Research has also shown that the development some mental illnesses, or the worsening of its symptoms, are linked to brain damage. It has been found that there is a strong link between the development of obsessive-compulsive disorder in children and a condition known as *pediatric autoimmune neuropsychiatric*. In this manner, the causes of abnormal behaviour/mental illnesses can be due to infections.

Prenatal Damage: There is a large body of evidence suggesting that a disruption of early fetal brain development or trauma that occurs at the time of birth due to loss of oxygen to the brain or any other reason may be a factor in the development of certain conditions. One such condition is autism.

Substance Abuse: Long-term substance abuse, in particular, has been linked to anxiety, depression, and paranoia. The question is what comes first – substance abuse or the mental health problem. The answer is that although disorders like anxiety and depression are closely linked with substance abuse but they are not responsible for the cause of the other. The only relationship that exists is that of the side effects of long-term substance abuse. When an individual resorts to substance abuse for seeking relief from the torments of the mental disorder, he does get temporary relief but in the end, this relief turns into agony by aggravating the symptoms. Thus alcohol and drug abuse push the individual over the edge making him more vulnerable. Substance abuse may also sharply increase symptoms of mental illness or trigger new ones. Alcohol and drug abuse also interact with medications such as antidepressants, anti-anxiety pills, and mood stabilizers making them less effective.

Other Factors: Other biological factors responsible for the development of mental illness may range from lack of proper nutrition for healthy development and growth of the body; exposure to toxins (such as lead) because of work or accident or proximity of the emission of toxins to the residential area. All such factors, which cause direct or indirect harm to the health of an individual, can be probable causes of abnormal behaviour.

PSYCHOSOCIAL FACTORS

There are many psychosocial and interpersonal factors, which play a significant role in maladaptive behaviours, and each of these factors, by no mean is independent of each other and that a given condition may function as a primary, pre-disposing, precipitating, or, reinforcing cause. We will now examine all such psychosocial and interpersonal factors in detail because they play a dominating role in the cause of development of abnormal behaviours.

Maternal Deprivation: Infants who are deprived of maternal stimulation either as a consequence of separation from the mother or placement in a boarding school at a very early age or lack adequate "mothering" at home are prone to develop many a personality and other mental disorders. In such cases the child is deprived of love and affection from his parents, especially from his/her mother and thus experiences less warmth and physical contact, less intellectual, emotional, and social stimulation and a lack of encouragement and help in positive learning.

This type of environment many a times leads to retarded intellect, emotional, social, and even physical development. As these children grow up, they find it difficult to form close interpersonal relationships and often exhibit antisocial behaviour.

Pathogenic Family Patterns: Home is the first school of a child. As an infant progress into childhood, he must master new competencies, learn usable assumptions about himself and the world, and exert increasing inner control over his behaviour. During this period, the family unit remains the crucial guiding influence in the child's personality development; unfortunately, faulty family patterns are a fertile source of unhealthy development and maladjustment.

Parental Rejection: Parents may reject their child by showing physical neglect, denial of love and affection, lack of interest in the child's activities, and achievements, harsh or inconsistent punishment, failure to spend time with the child, and lack of respect for the child's rights and feelings as a person. This parental rejection tends to foster, in the child, low self-esteem, and feelings of insecurity, increased aggression, loneliness, and inability to give and receive love.

Overprotection And Restrictiveness: On the other hand, over protectiveness and restrictiveness in the parents attitude may also be a source for development of personality disorders. In such families the child is not left free to develop on his own and made dependent for everything by his parents. He is to follow the code of conduct as laid down by his parents and not permitted to deviate from the same. Such an attitude of the parents though may lead to a well-controlled behaviour but it also tends to nature fear, dependency, submission, repressed hostility, and some dulling of intellectual strivings. Such children when they grow up find it difficult to face and cope with stressful situations leading to adopting maladaptive coping strategies.

Over-permissiveness And Indulgence: This attitude of parents tends to make the children spoiled, selfish, inconsiderate, rebellious, and demanding. These children tend to become antisocial, and exhibit aggressive behaviour. However, they readily form relationships with people but exploit them for personal gains.

Unrealistic Demands: Some parents place excessive pressure on their children to live up to their expectations and the children find little room for development as an independent person. If the child fails to live up to the expectations, he falls in his own eyes as well as those of others. He gets frustrated and self-devaluated.

Faulty Discipline: Over severe or harsh punishment may have a variety of harmful effects on the child including fear and hatred of the punishing person, little initiative or spontaneity, and less friendly feelings towards others. If over severe discipline is accompanied by rigid moral standards then, it may, results in a seriously repressed child who lacks spontaneity and warmth and devotes much effort towards controlling his own unacceptable impulses. Such children often subject themselves to severe self-recrimination and self-punishment for real or imagined misdeeds. They also may become rebellious and exhibit in socially deviant behaviours.

Communication Failure: Faulty patterns of communication between parents and children tend to make the child emotionally disturbed. Such parents discourage a child from asking questions thus failing to foster the information exchange essential for healthy personality development.

Undesirable Parental Models: Children tend to observe and imitate the behaviour of their parents, it is apparent that parental behaviour can have a highly beneficial or detrimental effect on the way a child learns to perceive, think, feel and act.

Maladaptive Family Structure: Maladaptive behaviour on the part of the child may be fostered by the general family environment as well as by the child's relationship with one or both parents.

The Inadequate Family: This type of family is unable to cope with the ordinary problems of family living. It lacks the resources, physical or psychological, for meeting demands with which most families can satisfactorily cope. Consequently, the inadequate family relies heavily on continued outside assistance and support in resolving its problems. Such families thus are unable to provide the child feelings of safety and security it needs, or adequately guide them in the development of essential competencies.

The Disturbed Family: Certain characteristics of such families are common and they negatively effect the personality development of the child. Such families may include parents who are fighting to maintain their own equilibrium and unable to give the child needed love and guidance. They may also expose the child to irrationality and faulty parental models and enmesh the child between their own emotional conflicts. Children from such families tend to develop feelings of insecurity and may have difficulty making and maintaining healthy relationships with others.

The Antisocial Family: When parents are engaged in behaviours that violate the norms of society, they are setting a bad example before their children. Children of such families tend to follow on the footsteps of their parents and indulge in antisocial activities freely.

The Disrupted Family: These families are not complete in the sense that either of the parents is not present. This condition may be the result of death, separation, divorce or some other reason. Children in such a family develop feelings of insecurity and rejection, which may be aggravated by conflicting loyalties and sometimes, by spoiling the child receives while staying with one or the other parent – maybe not the one he/she would prefer to be with.

Early Childhood Trauma: Most of us have had traumatic experiences that have temporarily shattered our feelings of security, adequacy, and worth and were important in influencing our later evaluation of our environment and ourselves. The after effects of such early traumatic experiences depend heavily on the support and reassurances given to the child by parents or other significant persons. This appears particularly important when the trauma involves an experience that arouses strong feelings of inadequacy and self-devaluation. A child exposed to repeated trauma, which keeps him off balance, is likely to show disruption in normal personality development. Thus, early trauma seems to have more far-reaching consequences than later one's, largely because critical evaluation, reflection, and self-defenses are not yet well developed in children.

SOCIO-CULTURAL FACTORS

In addition to the biological and psychosocial factors that are crucial for mental health there are conditions especially characteristic of our time and place in history that put stress, directly or indirectly, on most of us. These conditions, if not conducive, can either alone, or in association with, the biological and psychosocial ones, can be disastrous to ones mental health. We will examine each one of these briefly and see their relative effect on the individual.

War, Terrorism And Violence: Even though at times wars may be necessary for bringing stability and order in the world they either directly or indirectly became reasons for instability within individuals. This instability then leads to mental disability. Today we all live under a conscious or unconscious threat of being engulfed in a thermonuclear holocaust or becoming the target of a terrorist attack. We also live under the fearful shadow of uncertain violence not knowing when we will be struck. All these conscious or unconscious fears make us feel anxious and stressful and we end up paying a price for living in a world, which appears hostile and threatening through our maladaptive behaviours. Though it appears as if we are only guarding ourselves but the *defense mechanisms* we use have long-term harmful effects.

Group Prejudice And Discrimination: A prejudice is a preconceived belief, opinion, or judgment towards a group of people or a single individual because or race, social class, gender, ethnicity, social orientation, age, disability, political beliefs, religion, line of work or other personal characteristics. Most of us must have had the frustrating experience of not getting a job, or unable to get a contract, or admission in a school etc., because of discriminations based on caste, creed, race, religion and all its likes. Our frustrations in turn aggravate us leading to psychological problems ranging from stress, sleep disorders, fearful dreams, depression, and irritability and so on and so forth.

Economic And Employment Problems: Recession, inflation, unemployment, and job dissatisfaction are sources of stress for many people in our society. Such problems can give rise to maladaptive behaviours such as depression, anxiety, mental tension, suicide, and even crime. Such adverse conditions can also play hell in interpersonal relationships leading to impaired marital adjustment. These conditions if not conducive can be a source of maladaptive behaviours.

Accelerating Technologies And Social Change: Accelerating change in our contemporary world has played havoc with established norms and values. All facets of our lives are being directly affected by the rate and frequency of change as it is occurring today – our education, our jobs, our family lives, our leisure pursuits, our economic security, and our beliefs and values. Constantly we are trying to keep pace with them but they exert stress upon our resources leading to an *existential anxiety*. To enable us to keep pace with the social changes we are discarding old traditional norms and values to give way to newer ones. Unfortunately, these changes are accompanied by considerable turmoil and stress making us mentally unhealthy.

The causes of abnormal behaviour maybe one, many, or various combinations but they are all because of unhealthy situations and circumstances. It is not necessary that only the weak are susceptible to them. Nobody, as long as he moves about among the chaotic currents of life, is without trouble. Even though through pride one may be ever deceiving their selves but deep below the surface of the average conscience a still, small voice will constantly be telling them that something is out of tune. A good life is not a fixed state. It is not a state of virtue, or contentment, or nirvana, or happiness. It is not a condition in which, the individual is adjusted, fulfilled, or actualized. The good life is not a state of drive-reduction, or tension-reduction, or homeostasis. The good life is a process, not a state of being. It is a direction not a destination. A happy life cannot be without a measure of darkness, and the word happy would lose its meaning if it were not balanced by sadness. It is far better to take things as they come along with patience and composure. This is what life is all about – a bit of spice, a bit of pepper, sometimes sweet and sometimes biter. All together, constitute the basic ingredients of flavour in the journey called life.

Chapter 4

The Devil of Stress – Bust It

"Anything that places a demand on our time and energy produces stress. In addition, stress is created by thinking or worrying about these demands, because we spend time with this process, and because thinking about demands often results in psychological distress. Both positive and negative life events and expectations produce stress, although the psychological impact of most negative life events is greater. Stress is both psychological and physical".

"Stress is nothing more than a socially acceptable form of mental illness"

The single most important key to good mental health is avoiding worry, stress, and tension. Technically stress may not be classified as a psychological disorder but it is the underlying cause of many a psychological problems. It has been found that in India 70 per cent to 90 per cent of adults visit primary care physicians for stress-related problems. Stress appears to be like an iceberg with only its tip visible, seemingly harmless. What lies hidden below is a cause of concern and worry. We need to educate ourselves with the same to be able to cope better with psychological disorders or problems.

We have all heard about stress and have passed through many stressful situations. Stress makes us feel uncomfortable because we fail to cope effectively with life's situations. This failure in turn makes us devalue ourselves and we become psychological wrecks.

Life would be simple indeed, if one's biological and psychological needs were automatically gratified. However, there are many obstacles, both environmental and personal, that may interfere. Such obstacles place *adjustive demands* or *stress* on the individual.

WHAT IS STRESS

Stress is a characteristic physiological response to *stressors* – the agents that produce stress. Stress, is the body's way of rising to a challenge and preparing to meet such situations with focus, strength, stamina, and heightened alertness. If this stress is in excess then it can have a harmful effect on normal functioning, disturbing the physiological and psychological functioning of an individual. In medical terminology, stress has been defined as a disturbance in the body's homeostasis. This happens when an individual tries to cope with continual life changes.

THE PHYSIOLOGY OF STRESS

Whenever an individual confronts a challenging situation the brain prepares the body for taking a defensive action. It releases stress hormones, cortisone, and adrenaline, which raise the blood pressure, preparing the body to take appropriate action. This action can vary from running away or attacking the situation. If this action is one of attack then the hormones released in the blood get used up leading to reduction in stress levels. This reduced stress level positively affects many other stress related disorders. Stress becomes problematic when an individual adopts the escape mechanism by avoiding confronting the challenging situation. In such a case, with the passage of time, the stress hormones, which had been released in the blood, begin to negatively act upon the physiological system. The body begins to show signs of stress like increase in muscle tension, unfocussed anxiety, dizziness, and increased heartbeats.

Challenging situations are a part of everyday life and our body is in a constant state of alarm. If we escape from them then the cumulative affect can lead to both acute and chronic psychosomatic illnesses and weaken the immune system.

THE DIFFERENT TYPES OF STRESS

People experience different types of stress, which mainly are classified into four categories.

Eustress: This is a short-term stress and provides immediate strength. This type of stress arises when one is involved in physical activities, gets enthusiastic, or involved in creative works. Eustress is positive in nature, originating when motivation and inspiration is required. Players and athletes generally experience this type of stress before an event.

Distress: This is a negative type of stress and is a resultant of constant readjustments or alternations in routine activities. It leads to feelings of discomfort and unfamiliarity. When stress is intense, arrives, and disappears quickly, it is termed as *acute stress*. When stress is prolonged, existing for weeks, months, or even years it is termed as *chronic stress*. Generally, people whose lives are unstable or their routine, keeps changing now and then, are more prone to distress.

Hyperstress: This type of stress is the resultant of being driven or pushed beyond ones capabilities or potentials. Biting off more than what one can chew creates pressure on bodily resources making them crack. Individuals suffering from hyperstress are also hypersensitive. Even little things can trigger a strong emotional reaction. In today's world, many people from different occupations are known to be suffering from hyperstress.

Hypostress: This is opposite of hyperstress. It is the resultant of boredom or inactivity. Such people are often restless and uninspired. People who perform repetitive tasks generally experience this type of stress.

STRESS CHECKLIST

Let us evaluate ourselves with regards to the adjustive demands that we have so that we may be able to identify them and work to overcome or remove them.

This checklist has been developed by me to *roughly* get for you a measure of the level of your psychological stress, if any, and which could be one of the underlying causes of your unhealthy mental state apart from others. Read each statement carefully, understand it and honestly respond to one of the two options given before it. There is nothing right or wrong about the statement. Kindly be honest in your own interest. (*Note that this checklist is only a rough measure of your psychological stress*).

1. I do not have any clearly defined goals in life: *True/False.*
2. I have difficulty overcoming obstacles that come in the way while achieving what I want: *True/False.*
3. I have a lot of competition in the work that I do: *True/False.*
4. I have set too high goals for myself: *True/False.*
5. I am on the wrong side of life's track: *True/False.*
6. I am economically not well off. *True/False.*

7. I am not free to do what I want: *True/False.*
8. I lack charisma: *True/False.*
9. I am not emotionally stable: *True/False.*
10. I have limited scope for economic growth: *True/False.*
11. I have difficulty making choices: *True/False.*
12. I want to approach as well as avoid many situations: *True/False.*
13. I have difficulty choosing between two attractive alternatives: *True/False.*
14. It seems my life is caught between the devil and the deep blue sea: *True/False.*
15. I am under pressure of meeting deadlines most of the time: *True/False.*

SCORING AND INTERPRETATION

After you have responded to the above statements, assign a point of 0 to all the *false* you have marked and a point of 1 to all the *true* that you have marked. Total up your score. If your score lies in the range of 0 - 5 you have a *low stress level*; 6 - 10 you have a *moderate stress level* and if it lies in the range of 11 – 15 you are *highly stressed.*

FIND THE PSYCHOLOGICAL CAUSES OF YOUR STRESS

If you have high stress levels then look for the cause of the same amongst its various psychological causes. Identifying the source of your stress will help you cope better with it.

You May Be Frustrated: If you have scored high on the stress checklist it may be because you are frustrated. This frustration may be the resultant because some strivings of yours may have been thwarted either by obstacles that blocked your progress towards a desired goal or you may not be having any appropriate goal to achieve. The failure on your part to achieve your desired goal may be because you are not well-equipped to satisfy your desires. You may have set too high standards of achievement, which you could not achieve, or having difficulty to achieve. Others may be having too many expectations from you, which you are unable to fulfil. There is also a probability of social obstacles coming your way in fulfilling your desires, which may be unethical.

Any one of these factors may be causing frustration to you giving rise to stress.

You May Be Having Conflicts: In many instances, stress results from the necessity of choosing between two needs or goals. Usually the choice of one alternative means frustration with regards to the other. You may be in a situation where you want to approach as well as to avoid the same goal. Example: You want to get married but fear taking up the responsibilities of married life. You may be in a conflicting state because you want to approach two goals simultaneously but you have to choose one among them. Example: There may be two job openings for you and you are in a conflicting state which one to opt for. You may have been caught between the devil and the deep blue sea – wanting to avoid both situations but have to choose one out of them. Example: One may have to choose between finishing a job one dislikes or quitting and being called a failure.

You May Be Under Pressure: Your stress may have stemmed not only from frustrations and conflicts, but also from pressure to achieve particular goals or behave in particular ways. The source of such pressers may be located within you or your environment. Example: A sales executive may feel under severe pressure to meet the target because his promotion depends upon the same or he may submit himself to such pressure because he wants to rise higher in the organizational hierarchy. Pressure, in general, forces one to speed up, intensify, or change the direction of goal-oriented behaviour. You may be encountering different pressures in the course of everyday living, and often you must have handled them without much difficulty. However, in some cases the pressure may have seriously taxed your adjustive resources and become excessive leading to a breakdown of your organized behaviour thus resulting in stress.

TAMING THE DEVIL OF STRESS

The human brain is more like an elaborated communication, problem-solving and decision-making center where incoming information is continuously evaluated, alternative responses are formulated and weighed, decisions are made and implemented, and feedback is checked with a view to correcting possible errors. Making use of this God-gifted system one can effectively cope with situations and circumstances causing damage to the physical and mental self. There are a number of ways to effectively cope with the various adjustive demands. A few of them are being outlines.

Appraising The Stress Situation: When a new adjustive demand is perceived, your brain quickly assigns it to a particular category of problems. This is automatically done on the basis of similarities to and differences from previous such situations you may have encountered in the past. Your brain simultaneously also gauges the level of danger or threat posed by the problem at hand. If it finds the stress as a serious threat, it will make you feel anxious and interrupt your other ongoing activities in order to cope with the situation.

Take Decision and Solve The Problem: After the stress-arousing situation has been categorized by your brain appraise the same and formulate an alternate course of action using past experiences with similar situations. Along side, also assess the relative merits of alternative solutions and make a choice. The factors on which you can base your choice of action can be the probabilities of success, the degree of satisfaction you are willing to accept, and the cost you will be paying. In short, you have to strike a balance between probability, desirability, and cost.

Take Action and Use Feedback: Once you have taken a decision your next step should be to implement it – putting you plan into action. Once your plan of action has been embarked upon, you can keep checking on whatever feedback information is available to see if corrections or adjustments in ongoing actions are indicated and feasible. This can be done by abruptly terminating one course of action and the formulation and implementation of another that appears more likely to prove effective.

APPLYING COPING STRATEGIES

The first and most important thing in coping with any stressful situation is making a realistic analysis and then attempting a positive outcome. How are you going to do this? First, imagine the forthcoming event and concentrate on that event in its totality. This way you will have a clear picture worked out in your mind about it. After you have done so then specify your goals and if you anticipate an unpleasant situation then work out as to how you are going to react to it. This is planning including pre-evaluation and overcoming hurdles.

Now imagine the situation in your mind and rehearse fully how you are going to face it. Visualize yourself as going through the situation in a controlled, confident, and relaxed manner. This will ease the pressure out of you and drastically reduce your stress level.

You can take a break if the anticipation period becomes too tense. Indulge in some recreational activities. This will divert your thought and keep the problem at hand in the background. It will also help you to deal with the nervousness building up inside you and prevent you from getting tense.

After you have taken the required break, prepare yourself for the worst to happen and at the same time visualize yourself dealing with such a bad situation efficiently. This imaginary exercise will boost your level of confidence and you will feel that you can do it.

However, be realistic despite of all your preparations. Some amount of stress is still likely to be present, which is a positive thing. The fact is that some amount of stress is required for effective performance.

Keep giving yourself some positive strokes. It may not be possible to deal with every situation successfully. Whatever the degree of success, it deserves some kind of self–reward.

Reassess the situation and then revaluate the situation to see what you did well and where you went wrong. This reassessment helps in thinking of better strategies to deal with the situation in future.

A positive attitude works when it becomes a way of life. To become a part of your thought, plan, and action it must be practised continuously. Thus, if we want to be stress free and happy we must have a positive attitude. You must approach life's stressful situations with a positive pattern of thought. This positive thinking on our part will surely do wonders for our level of stress and thereby directly affect your mental health. So try to live stress free life and be happy. Nothing gives one person so much comfort as to remain always cool and unruffled under all circumstances. Your road to wellbeing will be less bumpy and smoother if you learn to bust your stress.

Chapter 5

The Devil of Mental Fatigue – Rest It

"A psychological disorder characterized especially by physical and mental exhaustion usually with accompanying symptoms (as headaches, insomnia, and irritability), is believed to result from psychological factors (as depression or emotional stress or conflict), and is sometimes considered similar to or identical with chronic fatigue syndrome".

"Our fatigue is often caused not by work, but by worry, frustration, and resentment"

To remain mentally healthy it is also essential to have some mental tension. If this is not so the mind, like any unused mechanical equipment, will gather rust. To ensure proper functioning of any machinery it is essential to keep it in use from time to time. This also applies to the mind. Thus, for the mind to function in a healthy and efficient manner it is essential for mental tension to be present within reasonable limits. This type of tension is referred to as beneficial tension or necessary tension. When this tension rises beyond the safety mark it becomes alarming and a cause to worry. Many people will confuse between mental tension and mental fatigue. Tension is actually a situation, and fatigues an ailment.

Some problem causing tension surrounds every individual. These problems can be related with either work, home or inter-personal relationships. If he fails in working out a solution to these problems and they persists for too long then they cause mental tension. This mental tension in the end gives rise to what is known as mental fatigue. In medical terminology, this mental fatigue is labeled as *Neurasthenia*. It is the result of exhaustion of the central nervous system's energy reserves, which is the resultant of stress caused in meeting the challenges of modern civilization.

Neurasthenia donates a condition with symptoms of fatigue, anxiety, headache, neuralgia, and depressed mood. Individuals suffering from neurasthenia feel lethargic, and show signs of irritability. They are unable to concentrate and worry a lot.

It is very difficult for even medical practitioners to detect and diagnose neurasthenia and thus this problem goes unattended. This is so because of the fact that the symptoms of neurasthenia are somewhat similar to that of depression, generalized anxiety disorder, somatic complains and other psychosomatic conditions. However, the catch in the diagnosis is that as in the case of these ailments, people suffering from neurasthenia generally do not go into a melancholy state – despair, sadness, gloominess, and misery. This is a hairline demarcation and very difficult to differentiate.

NEURASTHENIA – ARE YOU FATIGUED?

Take the following test to know your status on Neurasthenia. This test has been constructed based on the physical and mental symptoms associated with Neurasthenia. Remember that this is a rough measure of Neurasthenia and not intended for medical diagnosis. Read each statement carefully and then assign the "point" (0-3) in the blank space provided at the beginning of each statement. *The point you choose to assign is to be based on the frequency of occurrences with regards to the statement.*

Points

0 – Never.
1 – Sometimes.
2 – Most of the time.
3 – Always.

____ 1. I feel exhausted after doing minor tasks.
____ 2. I suffer from stomach ailments.
____ 3. I have muscles aches.
____ 4. I experience pain in my joints.
____ 5. I have headaches.
____ 6. I experience dizziness.
____ 7. My heart beats rapidly.
____ 8. I sweat a lot.

_____ 9. I experience a loss in my energy level.
_____ 10. My mouth becomes dry.
_____ 11. I experience pain in my waist.
_____ 12. I take long and deep breaths.
_____ 13. I have difficulty in concentrating.
_____ 14. I forget things.
_____ 15. I feel a decrease in my sexual drive.
_____ 16. I experience funny sensations in my hands and legs.
_____ 17. I have difficulty in sleeping.
_____ 18. I have a negative outlook towards things.
_____ 19. I feel irritated.
_____ 20. I feel heavy in the head.
_____ **Total Score**

SCORING AND INTERPRETATION

After you have assigned the points for each statement total them up. The total is your score on this measure. If you have scored in the range of 46 – 60, you exhibit *extremely high symptoms* of neurasthenia; in the range of 31 – 45, you exhibit *high symptoms*; in the range of 16 – 30, you exhibit some *moderate level of symptoms* and in the range of 0 -15 you are presently in the *safer zone* as far as neurasthenia is concerned.

Remember this is only an indicator to help you find out if you are suffering from neurasthenia. If you have scored extremely high or high, it is time that you take treatment and talk with your psychiatrist/clinical psychologist.

CAUSES OF NEURASTHENIA – FIND YOURS

If the mental tension increases unduly then the neurotransmitters begin to decrease the level of chemicals present in the veins of the brain. This in due course of time results in mental fatigue. Every individual can have different reasons for mental fatigue or neurasthenia. These symptoms are also common with many other physical and mental ailments. If you have scored high on the above measure, try finding your reasons from some listed below.

You May Be In A Hurry To Achieve Success: Who does not want to be successful and those who are in a hurry to achieve success invite their share of problems – physical as well as mental. Working towards the achievement of a goal exerts pressure on our physical and psychological resources. Our body can cope well if the pressure exerted is well within its capacity to handle. If the pressure becomes in excess then it leads to quick combustion and thereby exhaustion of the central nervous system's energy reserves of resources. An athlete running a marathon does not take a sprint right from the outset. He maintains a steady speed for most part of the race and nearing the final point accelerates. He uses his body energy reserves in a proper manner, exerting the maximum force at the end of the race, where thereafter he can rest and recoup his energies. So watch out if you have been in a hurry to win a life's marathon. Save your energies for the time you will require them the most. Remember slow and steady wins the race.

Your Society May Be The Source of Your Problems: India is a culturally and traditionally rich nation but this very richness has become a cause of concern for the modern generation. Most of us Indians have been brought up being educated about the value systems but unfortunately, we perceive them as traditional shackles and do not want to be chained down with them. We want our freedom to live life the way we want. On the other hand, we wish that people around us follow the moralistic and traditional code of conduct and behave according to societal norms. In short, we feel that all laws and rules are made for others to follow. This state of thinking makes us conflicting personalities, generating within us various complexities, which only aggravate our tensions and slowly lead to our suffering from neurasthenia and other psychological ailments. If this is the case with you remember that it is the individual, which makes the society, and if its complexities are causing you problems, then you have to first mend your ways. Either you learn to ignore what society demands and stop expecting others to follow social norms or you follow social norms and stop bothering about others. In short live your life and let others live theirs.

You May Be Having Problems Handling Inter-Personal Relationships: Your mental fatigue may be the outcome of ongoing conflicts and tensions in your relationships. These relationships may be personal, professional – ethical or unethical. Healthy relationships give a positive boost to one's mental health but problems within them give rise to worries and tensions. These worries and tensions may not be apparently visible but they are there deep down within the unconscious, casting their shadow of gloom and despair. This state of the mind fatigues it and before you know, you are a patient of some mental ailment. Sort out your inter-personal problems and finish them finally before they end up finishing you. If a relationship cannot be worked out, then either break it or stop bothering about it. You have to learn to develop a healthy relation with your own self.

You May Be Having High Expectations From Your Own Self: Many a time's neurasthenia is the resultant of high expectations. High expectations from others who matter in your life are sometimes understandable because they mistakenly overestimate your potentials. However, when you yourself, being aware of your limited potentials, begin dreaming of achieving the impossible you end up acquiring nothing but a bundle of problems for yourself – neurasthenia is just one small part of it. If you have scored high on the above measure it is time that you reassess your potentials and take on tasks, which you can, comfortablly accomplish. Being true to your self is the master key to good mental health.

You May Be Facing Economic Problems: Psychological problems are generally the outcome of biological, psychosocial, and economic reasons. Facing financial hardships can cause great damage to self and family. If one is unable to meet his basic needs and/or satisfy the needs of his family then it becomes a cause of great concern. Many families across the world have committed suicide because of economic reasons. If you are having tensions because of economic reasons and exhibiting symptoms of neurasthenia then my advice to you is to face the present situation with courage. Bad times do pass away and so will this situation. Remember not to grow bigger than your boot. All one needs to survive is the fulfillment of the basic biological needs of food, clothing, and shelter. The needs for safety and security, love, belonging and affection follow suite. Restrict your baseless needs because your mental health is of prime importance.

You May Be Under Pressure From Different Quarters: Pressure of any kind can give tensions and fatigue our mental faculty. The source of pressure can be from family, friends, or even enemies. Sometimes we ourselves create pressure. If you are under any type of pressure then take it off your back. The pressure, if present constantly will not let you act efficiently and your efforts will not be rewarded in their totality. Working under pressure is strenuous and harmful to the nervous system, which if malfunctions, can lead to many ailments. Therefore, it is best to puncture your pressure and take the excess air out! Also, remember you cannot run your vehicle on a flat tyre. You do need some pressure for healthy execution of activities.

TAMING THE DEVIL OF NEURASTHENIA

After having gone thorough, the neurasthenia measure if you feel that you suffer from the same its best advised to visit a medical practitioner or a clinical psychologist for advice. Along side, you can also help yourself in controlling the situation by following the coping strategies listed below. Remember practice makes a man perfect but it takes time to practise and achieve perfection. Follow these coping strategies with patience and determination and they will bring positive results in due course of time.

Practise Relaxation: Relaxation therapy is the body's natural relaxation response, a powerful antidote to stress. Relaxation techniques such as deep breathing, visualization, progressive muscle relaxation, meditation, and yoga can help you activate this relaxation response. When practised regularly, these activities lead to a reduction in your everyday stress levels and a boost in your feelings of joy and serenity. What's more, they also serve a protective quality by teaching you how to stay calm and collected in the face of life's curveballs. (*Explained in detail in chapter on Relaxation Therapy*).

Serialize Your Problems: One way to avoid tensions and thereby other related disorders is to write down your problems on a piece of paper beginning with the recent and crucial ones. Doing so will set for you a priority order for attending to them. Take up the issues one by one and try sorting them out. If you by chance fail at any one move to the other in the list. Do not sit and brood over what you could not work out. Brooding will only complicate matters for you and you will end up with more problems on your list.

Leave Some Problems To Be Solved At A Latter Stage: There is a time for every thing. If you are searching for mangoes in winters, they are not going to be available easily. You will have to visit many places or cities before you get them. This will bring undue stress upon you. If you want to eat mangoes its best that you wait for its season to come. The same is with problems. Many times we worry about things or try achieving those, which are present in the future and not available in the present. A father may begin to be troubled by the thought of his daughter's marriage who presently is just ten years old. In addition, many times we try solving out things, which do not happen to work out at that very moment. It is best for us to put off our efforts for sometime and try again at a latter stage when things appear favourable. Patience is the name of fruitful problem solving.

Do Not Sit Idle: An empty mind is a devils workshop. This workshop when idle begins to generate many thoughts, which mostly are negative in nature and harmful for your health. Engage your time in constructive activities such that your energies may be diverted and utilized for your betterment. You can also spend time attending to your hobbies or any other recreational activities. In short, you have to make constructive and effective use of you energies.

Think Positively: Remember you are what you think. It is your thought, which makes you or breaks you. If you perceive situations and events in a negative manner, you will be adding fuel to fire. These negative approaches will in due course of time condition your thought pattern and you will end up looking at most of the things in a negative fashion. Learn to look for the positive side into things and use them to your advantage. In short, develop positive thinking.

Many people adapt to the situation when they find that they will be unable to cope up with the pressures exerted in meeting the challenges of the situation. Such people are intelligent and their adaptive mechanisms well equipped. They are good judges and know when it is time to withdraw, thus avoiding the self from hurt and disintegration. Some on the other hand cannot weigh the pros and cons of a situation and go around exerting their resources only to find themselves exhausted in the end. Such people generally end up with several mental ailments the core of which is mental fatigue. Now the choice rests upon you, your intelligence to be able to discriminate what can, and what cannot be changed. What you can you should and what you cannot you should accept. Avoid being unduly fatigues; use your energies in a planned and constructive manner.

Chapter 6

The Devil of Panic Attacks – Calm It Down

"A panic attack is a sudden, intense experience of fear coupled with an overwhelming feeling of danger, accompanied by physical symptoms of anxiety, such as a pounding heart, sweating, and rapid breathing. A person with panic disorder may have repeated panic attacks (at least several a month) and feel severe anxiety about having another attack".

"Panic is a sudden desertion of us, and a going over to the enemy of our imagination."

Panic attacks are linked to panic disorders, which are rooted in anxiety disorders. If you exhibit symptoms of panic disorders and recognize them then you should be relieved since they are making you aware of your anxiety. This is advantageous in helping you to treat your anxiety attacks.

Panic attacks surface suddenly accompanied with feelings of intense anxiety, heightened physiological arousal, fear, stomach problems, and uneasiness that is linked with a variety of other disorders. Imagine coming across a dreadful looking stray dog while taking a morning walk. The dog may not be even looking directly at you but you begin to sweat and trembling, find it difficult to breath, your heart begins to palpitate, and so on. You will then either run away or shoo the dog away. Many people experience panic attacks for no reason and its fear may prevent them from carrying out even simple daily routines – shopping or pillion riding a two-wheeler.

DO YOU HAVE PANIC ATTACKS?

The following measure will help you evaluate your vulnerability to panic attacks. Respond to the questions honestly, because the results will provide help to you in controlling your mental health since panic disorders often go hand in hand with other psychological disorders like depression, obsessive-compulsive disorder, suicidal thoughts, and even physical health complaints.

Task: *Imagine any one of the following situations you may have been in or any other similar situations you have experienced in the* *recent past*: Appearing for a surprise test, Annual exams, Power failure a day before your exam, Getting late to catch your flight/train, Result declaration, Just before facing an interview, Asked to give a speech without prior information, Learning new tasks, Approaching a stranger for a talk, Before meeting big people, Suddenly asked to take up a big responsibility, Just before a matrimonial alliance meeting with future partner, etc.

Note: *If you are imagining the situation then kindly do so with an intense feeling trying to make the situation realistic. If you have been in any such situation in the past then base your responses on its recollection.*

1. Did your heart beat suddenly increase/heart palpitate / ponder? Yes/No.
2. Did you suddenly begin to sweat? Yes/No.
3. Did you body begin to tremble? Yes/No.
4. Did you have sudden breathing problems – shortness of breath, suffocation? Yes/No.
5. Did you experience a feeling of choking? Yes/No.
6. Did you have pain in the chest? Yes/No.
7. Did you have feelings of nausea? Yes/No.
8. Did you experience discomfort in the stomach region? Yes/No.
9. Did you feel dizzy? Yes/No.
10. Did you experience feelings of unreality? Yes/No.
11. Did you feel detached from yourself? Yes/No.
12. Did you fear that you would loose control or go crazy? Yes/No.
13. Did you feel as if you were dying? Yes/No.
14. Did you feel numbness or tingling sensations in your body parts? Yes/No.
15. Did you feel chills or hot flashes? Yes/No.

SCORING AND INTERPRETATION

Kindly note this is not a diagnostic test and the obtained scores are hypothetical. This measure only guides you in knowing whether you are prone to panic attacks.

After having marked your responses, assign a point of 1 to every Yes. Total it up. This is your score on this measure. If your score lies, in the range of 11 – 15 you exhibit *high symptoms* of panic attacks; 6 - 10 you exhibit *moderate symptoms of panic attacks* and if it lies in the range of 0 – 5 you do not appear to be bothered by panic attacks.

Before suggesting remedies to handle panic situations, let us develop awareness about the symptoms and causes of panic attacks. This information will help you cope better in handling panic attacks if you are having them.

SYMPTOMS OF PANIC ATTACKS

Since a panic attack is sudden and commonly lasts approximately between periods of 15 seconds to 30 minutes, its symptoms die out with the passage of time. However, sometimes these attacks may form a cyclic series of episodes, lasting for an extended period, but not more than a few hours. The symptoms of panic attack may show as if the body is failing but in fact, it is protecting itself from harm. A panic attack begins with little provoking stimulus which generally onsets the feeling of fear. The body then releases the hormone *epinephrine*, which makes the individual to run away from the situation or attack it. In either case, the body is preparing itself for a strenuous physical activity.

After these hidden physiological reactions, there appear symptoms, which can be classified, into *beneficial* and *harmful*. However, the beneficial symptoms ultimately end up causing harm only.

BENEFICIAL SYMPTOMS

1. Increased heart rate – heart pumps more blood to the external organs and muscles for action.
2. Rapid breathing, perceived as shortness of breath – more oxygen supply for quick combustion and thereby energy release.
3. Sweating – this increases grip and helps heat loss.

HARMFUL SYMPTOMS

Though the body has prepared itself for strenuous activities, they rarely follow. The rapid breathing, which has dropped carbon dioxide levels in the lung and blood, leads to shifts in the blood pH. This in turn often leads to the following harmful effects:

1. Tingling or numbness - due to shifts in blood pH
2. Dizziness – due to less blood flow to the head.
3. Lightheadedness – due to less blood flow to the head.
4. Reduction in blood sugar level – it has been directed to the major muscles.

OTHER PHYSICAL SYMPTOMS

1. Feeling of choking.
2. Trembling or shaking.
3. Chest pain or discomfort.
4. Nausea or abdominal distress.
5. Feelings of unreality.
6. Feeling detached from oneself.
7. Fear of loosing control or going crazy.
8. Fear of dying.
9. Chills or hot flashes.

CAUSES OF PANIC ATTACKS: FIND YOURS AND TAME THIS DEVIL

1. **It May Be In Your Genes:** Research has shown that panic disorders can be genetically transmitted. However, it is also evident that people with no family history of panic attacks also develop this disorder. If you have scored high on the panic measure then check out you family history maybe you have inherited the same. Remember you can gain control over yourself and learn to tactfully handle panic attacks. If your attacks are making your life miserable, visit your psychiatrist/ clinical psychologist for medication and therapy. You can be cured.
2. **You May Have Acquired It From Your Environment**: People who do not inherit panic disorders but suffer from the same may acquire it from family or friends. Many parents are known to impress upon their children to be overly cautious in doing tasks, dealing with people, or handling situations

requiring skills. Such a cautious attitude over time results in the production of stress, which leads to panic attacks. If your panic score is high, it may be because of your faulty upbringing. You can change the way you have been taught to handle situations and things. Exercising caution is good but in excess, it is harmful. Change your outlook and freely approach events and situations with self-confidence. You can handle them better without panic. Check chapter on anxiety and find detail strategies of coping.

3. **There May Be A Biological Cause**: The source of panic disorders can also be biological. Many disorders are interrelated and influence each other. They also exhibit many common symptoms. If you have scored, high on the panic measure then may be you suffer from one or more of the related disorders. Do not worry since this is only an assumption based on your responses to panic situations and no specific statement can be made unless proper clinical diagnosis is done. Consult your psychiatrist/clinical psychologist and get a proper diagnosis.
4. **You May Be Suffering From Some Phobia**: Many people experience panic attacks as a direct result of exposure to a phobic object or situation. If you exhibit symptoms of panic attacks then evaluate your phobias if any. They may be influencing your panic attacks. Scare your phobias. Read beyond for assistance on phobias.
5. **Your Life Situations/Life-Style May Be Triggering Your Panic Attacks**: Panic attacks can also be triggered by major personal loss like emotional attachments to a romantic partner, major life changes, and life transitions. Drugs such as psilocybin and marijuana and stimulants such as nicotine and caffeine can also trigger panic attacks. Look at your recent past and present life and check your stimulant/drug usages. You may be able to locate you panic trigger.
6. **You May Be Maintaining The Source of Your Panics**: Many of our actions assist in maintaining what we should eradicate from our psyche. We knowingly avoid panic provoking situations or environments, get anxious, and indulge in negative self-talk. We harbour mistaken beliefs, which turn

nervousness into panic. We also withhold our feelings and bottle them up. All these negative personality traits only assist in aggravating our panic. If you fall in this category then mend your ways before it gets too late.

7. **You May Be Lacking Assertiveness**: Research has shown that those who suffer from panic attacks engage in a passive style of communication or interaction with others. However, this style of communication is surely polite and respectful it is characteristically unassertive. This unassertive style, by its constant presence, contributes to panic attacks in those who are troubled with it. Learn to be assertive it will boost your self-confidence, driving your panic away.
8. **Your Panic Attacks May Be The Side Effects of Ongoing Medications**: Some types of antibiotics or other medications are known to be sources of temporarily triggering panic attacks. Some antidepressants drugs can also cause increased anxiety in the beginning of their use. If you are having panic, attacks and are on any type of medication then check with your doctor.
9. **Withdrawal From Drugs, Medication, or Alcohol Can Cause Panic Attacks**: If you have recently quit any types of drugs – prescribed or un-prescribed, quit or reduced your alcohol intake and experiencing panic attacks then do not worry. The attacks are part of their withdrawal syndrome or rebound effect. Stick to your withdrawal and say no to alcohol and un-prescribed drugs.
10. **Your Breathing Style May Cause Panic Attacks**: If you are in a habit of breathing from the chest it may be causing you over breathing. You exhale more carbon dioxide in relation to the amount of oxygen you have in your bloodstream. This leads to respiratory alkalosis and hypocapnia. This leads to the exhibition of symptoms like rapid heartbeat, tingling or numbness, dizziness, burning and lightheadedness, which can trigger panic attacks. This syndrome also often involves prominent mouth breathing. If this syndrome is the cause of your panic attack then learn to breathe through your nose.

11. **Your Past Experience Can Be The Source of Your Panic Attacks**: It is normal to evaluate a present situation on the basis of past experience in similar situations. However, if you have not had a positive experience in the past under such a situation your evaluation will give rise to panic. The continued encounter with this specific situation in the future will condition the panic response and whenever such a situation arises, it will generate a panic attack. If this is the case with you then remember you can change things if you handle the specific situation with a different approach and calmness.
12. **Your Poor Health Can Be Causes of Your Panic Attacks**: If you suffer from heart ailments, Wolff-Parkinson-White syndrome, or any such ailment that necessitates emergency medical attention at any unknown time then you have enough cause to have panic attacks. You panic at the mere thought of what will happen if I need medical attention in the early hours of the morning, are caught in a traffic jam while being rushed to hospital during peak hours and so on, and so forth. If you are suffering from any such medical problems, your panic will only worsen your condition. Stop thinking and enjoy the present to the fullest.

Panic disorders often goes hand-in-hand with other psychological disorders, like depression, alcohol abuse, obsessive-compulsive disorder, suicidal thoughts, and even physical health complaints. Overcoming panic disorders and panic attacks is almost successful. Its treatment varies from person to person and ranges from psychotherapy and mild medication. The best possible way is perceptual alternation – changing your perspective positively towards previously negative panic arousing situations and events. Changing this will influence your thinking and that in turn will make you take a positive step towards bravely taking on the task, which threatened you. Panic is the outcome of a negative mind set which has to be altered and only you can do it. Try it to believe me.

Chapter 7

The Devil of Anxiety – A Boon or Disorder

"We have all experienced significant anxiety at one time or another, although perhaps not severe enough to warrant a diagnosis by a professional. Anxiety is a danger or an alert signal. The physiological arousal we experience as anxiety is directly related to fear of harm. When we are faced with a threat to our physical well-being that can result in either serious physical harm or death, we respond psychologically and physically. This response has been called the "fight or flight" response because it activates us to either defend ourselves, or to run away and escape injury. In a life threatening crisis, this fight or flight response can save our lives".

"It has been said that our anxiety does not empty tomorrow of its sorrow, but only empties today of its strength".

Many a gifted and intellectual people are unable to bring to utilization their full potentials because of a constant fear of worrying about mostly what does not exist in the present. It is roughly estimated that every one out of twenty Indians suffer from such kinds of a disorder technically known as *anxiety*.

You will be surprised to know that anxiety is both a boon as well as a disorder. What decides its significance is its level. It is a boon when present in normal level, a disorder when it is high and disadvantageous when low or absent. For any individual to function normally and achieve his goals one has to be anxious about attaining them. It is this anxiety, which provides the driving force. If anxiety is at a normal level then the force exerted by it is beneficial but if the level of anxiety is high it hampers normal functioning leading to behavioural problems. If anxiety is very low or absent there will be no driving force. The individual will not work towards the attainment of his goals.

How anxious an individual will become depends largely upon his personality constitution. Some people are anxious by nature and even simple things create anxiety for them. This type of anxiety is a specific characteristic of their trait and aptly referred to as *trait anxiety*. Some people on the other hand suffer from pangs of anxiety depending upon situations and circumstances. This is referred to as *state anxiety*.

Anxiety can be either a short-term "state" or a long-term "trait." Trait anxiety reflects a stable tendency to respond with state anxiety in the anticipation of threatening situations. It is closely related to the personality trait of neuroticism.

HOW DOES ANXIETY ARISE?

Anxiety reactions reflect individual's acute feelings of inadequacy in the face of inner and outer stress perceived as threatening. Such reactions are considered normal when the stress situation is sufficiently severe to justify them. Anxiety becomes neurotic and considered pathological when it is elicited by stress situations that an average individual handles without much difficulty.

MEASURE YOUR LEVEL OF ANXIETY

Taking the following test will make you aware of your present level of anxiety. The statements are based on symptoms, which people suffering from anxiety exhibit. Being honest in your responses will only help you. Remember that this is only a rough measure of your anxiety and not a medical test.

Read each statement carefully and then assign the "point" (0-3) in the blank space provided at the beginning of each statement. *The point you choose to assign is to be based on the frequency of occurrences with regards to the statement.*

Points

0 – Never.
1 – Sometimes.
2 – Most of the time.
3 – Always.

____ 1. I have difficulty to concentrate on anything
____ 2. I have difficulty in making decisions.
____ 3. I cannot sleep well during the night.
____ 4. I sweat a lot.
____ 5. My muscles remain in a tensed state.
____ 6. I remain in a state of tension.
____ 7. I worry a lot.
____ 8. I feel uneasy.
____ 9. I am sensitive in interpersonal relationships.
____ 10. I feel inadequate.

_____ 11. I feel depressed.
_____ 12. I do not take decisions fearing I may make a mistake.
_____ 13. My postural movements are strained.
_____ 14. I over react to sudden or unexpected things.
_____ 15. I shake my legs when sitting.
_____ 16. I feel tension in my muscular regions.
_____ 17. I profusely perspire in the palms.
_____ 18. My blood pressure is high.
_____ 19. I suffer from heart palpitations.
_____ 20. After taking any decision, I wonder about its appropriateness.
_____ 21. I review my mistakes.
_____ 22. The past, present and future keeps worrying me.
_____ 23. I have nightmares.
_____ 24. I have feelings of imminent death.
_____ 25. I get fatigued very soon.
_____ 26. I keep moving around in the house aimlessly.
_____ 27. I am bothered by negative thoughts.
_____ 28. My outlook is pessimistic.
_____ 29. Small sounds startle me.
_____ 30. I suffer from stomach upsets.
_____ **Total Score**

SCORING AND INTERPRETATION

After you have assigned the points to each statement total them up. This will be your score on this measure. If you have scored in the range of 68 – 90, you are suffering from *extremely high anxiety*. If you have scored in the range of 46 - 67, you have a *high average anxiety*. If your have scored in the range of 23 – 45 you have a *normal average anxiety level*. If you have scored in the range of 0 – 22 then you have *low anxiety*.

Remember this is only an indicator to help you find out if you are suffering from anxiety. If you have scored high or extremely high, it is time that you take treatment and talk with your psychiatrist/clinical psychologist.

CAUSES OF ANXIETY DISORDERS – FIND YOURS

Having gone through every questions of the test you must have become aware of the symptoms of anxiety. What you now need to know is what causes anxiety. Causes of anxiety disorders range from genetics to chronic insomnia. Once the cause of an anxiety disorder is established, the treatment may be more effective.

1. **Childhood Experiences Can Be A Crucial Factor**: The total personality of an individual is determined by genetics, influenced, and shaped by the environment. Faulty parenting styles can lead to development of anxiety in the child. Faulty parenting may include undue criticism, very high expectations, perfectionism, and strict discipline among various other things. Parents, who do not provide a secure and conducive environment to their child, unknowingly, develop within him feelings of insecurity and inadequacy leading to anxiety. With the passage of time, this anxiety becomes a part of his lifestyle.
2. **Sleep Disturbances Can Cause Anxiety**: For a body to function in its normal state adequate sleep is essential. If a person is not able to have adequate sleep or has disturbed sleep, he is susceptible to both anxiety and depression. The interesting part is that sleep disturbances are also a symptom of anxiety as well as a cause. Inadequate sleep can cause stress, which in turn leads to anxiety. Research has shown that insomnia when treated alleviates feelings of anxiousness.
3. **Stress Can Cause Anxiety**: Stress both physical and mental is one crucial factor, which leads to creation of anxiety. This stress can be the resultant of stressful life situations such as the death of a loved one, a transfer, separation, or divorce. Other stressful events can be legal problems, ailments, economic problems, and problematic interpersonal relationships.
4. **Traumatic Experiences Can Cause Anxiety**: Many a times one experiences some trauma or the other. Depending on the constitutional makeup, the aftermath of such experience can be varied. An accident, an assault, witnessing a murder,

or experiencing hostility can create anxiety. This experience hunts in the form of nightmares, distressing thoughts, flashbacks, and emotional numbness, which are all symptoms of anxiety.

5. **Anxiety Can Be Transmitted**: There is some evidence to show that anxiety disorders have a genetic link. Parents who have anxiety disorders are found to have transmitted this trait to their offsprings. However, this transmission may also have occurred at the point of child rearing. A tense and anxious mother can transmit her anxiety to even a very young infant. A child who is exposed to faulty parental interaction soon may learn anxiety reactions similar to those of his parents.
6. **Chemical Imbalances Can Cause Anxiety**: Medical science has shown that, as in the case of depression, anxiety disorders can also be the resultant of imbalanced brain chemicals. This fact has been proved by the administration of recreational drugs, which change the balance of brain chemicals, to normal individuals. These administrations have led to high levels of anxiety or even panic attacks.
7. **Some Physical Diseases Can Lead To Anxiety**: As in the case of depression, ones ailment or deteriorating physical health may be the cause of anxiety.
8. **Unexpressed Feelings Can Cause Anxiety**: If one does not express his feelings, especially hostile ones, they became the cause of anxiety.
9. **Mistaken Beliefs**: Mistaken or irrational beliefs are truly mistaken or irrational because they fly in the face of reality. They set up expectations, which are unrealistic, thus causing emotional upset when the expectations are not met. The more rigid the mistaken belief, the more emotional upsets they produce. In short, mistaken beliefs turn irritation into rage, sadness into depression, and appropriate nervousness into anxiety and panic.
10. **Anxiety Can Be The Resultant of Lack of Self-Care**: People who do not take proper care about their physical and mental wellbeing are prone to anxiety disorders. A healthy mind stays

in a healthy body and if this abode is not maintained and taken care of, it will surely crack under stressful situations giving rise to anxiety.

11. **Flamboyant Life Styles Can Cause Anxiety**: Maintaining a flamboyant life style is not easy and it exerts a lot of stress on bodily resources. This stress in turn very often leads to anxiety.

DON'T WORRY BE HAPPY

Do not worry be happy because it is worrying which characterizes the generalized anxiety disorder. If you stop worrying, you will be freed of many psychological miseries. Worry fragments the mind, shatters focus, distorts perspective, and destroys inner ease. Worry is self-afflicted distress. It has no consistent practical outcome. When you learn how to stop worrying, you center your mind and adopt a single-minded focus. When you stop obsessive thinking patterns, you build inner peace and a relaxed mood.

Identify the insecurities within and around you. Some may be real and most of them imaginary. Work out solutions for the real ones and forget the unreal ones. Insecurities generally arise due to lack of faith in us. We feel inadequate in handling the difficult situations in life. We begin to worry about our future. We give up our struggles and quit. Do not quit. Handle the present with confidence and future will take care of itself.

TAMING THE DEVIL OF ANXIETY

If you have scored high on the anxiety measure, it is very important for you to cope with the same. Below are several major coping styles that you can apply to improve how to tackle your anxiety

1. **Restore Confidence In Yourself**: Many a time's anxiety surfaces when we have lost faith in our competencies. We begin to worry at each step and stage of the task we are involved. Develop a positive outlook towards the task, which is making you anxious, plan, and then execute systematically. Time spent in this constructive process will enable you to gather your self-confidence and drive your anxiety away.

2. **Get Hold of Yourself**: We have experienced that when confronted with stress arousing situations our nervousness gets the better of us. It is time that you should know one fact - stressful situations make even the strongest of individuals nervous. The secret of success lies in the ability to overcome this anxious state and gracefully perform the task. You have to hold yourself together and face tough situations with composure.
3. **Locate The Source of Your Anxiety**: Many people suffering from generalized anxiety disorder find it hard to locate or identify the anxiety-arousing stimulus. In many cases, the stimulus is not present in reality and is imaginary. In some cases, people develop a fear of facing it if identified hence resort to avoidance behaviour. Some on the other hand do not try locating the source fearing what it could possibly be. Such type of escapism or avoidance behaviour in fact acts as a catalyst enhancing the levels of anxiety. The best way to tackle anxiety situations is to be honest with yourself, search for the underlying causes, and confront them with a confidence. This exercise will also educate you about the reality of the anxiety-arousing situation – whether it is real or imaginary.
4. **Take Action**: Normal level of anxiety compels us to take action and solve the problem. This action on our part diffuses the anxiety. If anxiety levels are high then also to reduce it action must be taken. A problem exists because a solution for the same is there. Without a solution, a problem has no existence of its own. It is when things get complicated they turn into problems. Try different methods and approaches in trying to solve your problems. Flexibility is the master key to solutions. Do not give up on problem solving tasks. You surely will succeed. However, many a times one is confronted with such problematic situations which cannot be solved by simple action on our part. To successfully handle such situations one has to make use of past experiences and if possible seek help from others. What is ultimately important is that the anxiety-

arousing situation should be dealt with and the mission accomplished.

5. **Problems Pass Away With Time**: Nothing is ever permanent because time always keeps moving on. Your problems today will either be resolved of will become outdated. There will be new things to focus your attention on and newer problems also to solve. All you need is the serenity to accept the things you cannot change, courage to change the things you can and above all wisdom to know the difference.
6. **Yoga, Aerobics, or Simple Exercises Can Help**: Relaxation therapy is an important tool of the clinical psychologist but you can also learn to relax on your own. You should learn yoga or aerobics and find time to do the same. Yogic exercises will not only relax your muscles but its mindfulness meditation will also calm your mind. Aerobics and simple exercises will keep your physical body in shape. Thus, you physiological and psychological components are freed of stress and you are energized to tackle and deal efficiently with stressful situations.

People suffering from anxiety often find some relief with prescribed mild tranquilizers. However, this type of medication does not in any way help in modifying their life-style. Psychotherapy on the other hand is very helpful. It is directed at helping such people to discriminate between real and imagined dangers, to help learn more effective coping methods, and modify conditions in the life situation, which are serving to maintain the maladaptive behaviour. If you have a high level of anxiety, it will be best to see your psychotherapist.

Chapter 8

The Devil of Depression – Drive it Away

"I doubt completely my ability to do anything well. It seems as though my mind has slowed down and burned out to the point of being virtually useless. I am haunted with the desperate hopelessness of it all. Others say, "It's only temporary, it will pass, you will get over it," but of course they have not any idea of how I feel, although they are certain they do. If I cannot feel, move, think, or care, then what on earth is the point"?

"You largely constructed your depression. It was not given to you. Therefore, you can deconstruct it".

All of us have the blues sometimes and may become greatly depressed at the death of a loved one, a disappointment in love, an accident, some occupational setback, or feelings of guilt concerning failure or unethical desire or behaviour. If such distressing situations occur in our lives, we react with more than the usual amount of sadness and dejection and often fail to return to normal after a reasonable period. Such reactions on our part may last for weeks or even months but eventually clear up. However, in some cases, a mildly depressed mood remains after more severe symptoms have faded away.

Before we further talk about depression let us first find out your level of depression. I have roughly constructed the following scale for helping you to measure your depression level at the *present point of time*. Respond truthfully to the statements if you want this book to help you have a mentally healthy life.

MEASURE YOUR DEPRESSION LEVEL

This is a measure to assess your level of depression. Read each statement carefully and then assign the "point" (0-3) in the blank space provided at the beginning of each statement. *The point you choose to assign is to be based on the frequency with which you display the characteristic traits in the statement.*

Ratings

0 – Never.

1 – Sometimes.

2 – Most of the time.

3 – Always.

_____ 1. I remain sad.

_____ 2. Things, which were appealing in the past, now seem to disinterest me.

_____ 3. I do not feel like socializing with my friends.

_____ 4. I have a feeling that all good things in my life have ended.

_____ 5. I tend to forget even simple things.

_____ 6. I am besieged by the fear of my own death.

_____ 7. I experience physical discomfort.

_____ 8. I feel that I will be unable to perform those tasks, which I had performed with perfection in the past.

_____ 9. The feeling that I am useless overwhelms me.

_____ 10. I am unable to concentrate on anything I do.

_____ 11. I get irritated very easily.

_____ 12. I have panic attacks.

_____ 13. I am burdened by feelings of guilt.

_____ 14. I am obsessed by the thought of committing suicide.

_____ 15. I have difficulty in going to sleep.

SCORING AND INTERPRETATION

After you have assigned the points total them up. This is your score on this measure.

If you have scored in the range of 34 - 45, you are *highly depressed*. If your score is in the range of 23 – 33, you are *moderately depressed*. If it lies in the range, of 11 - 22, you are *mildly depressed* and in the range of 0 – 10 you do not seem to suffer from depression at this point of time.

Remember this is only an indicator to help you find out if you are depressed. If you have scored high or moderately it is time that you take treatment and talk with your psychiatrist/clinical psychologist.

Note: ***The outcome of this test is dependent upon your present set of circumstances and the results obtained need not be generalized for the future***. You may be depressed at this point of time but if you handle the situation well you may come out of your depressive mood.

ARE YOU DEPRESSED? FIND THE REASON AND OVERCOME IT

With the advancement of science and technology life may seem to look comfortable and happy for those who can afford its luxury and uncomfortable and unhappy for those who cannot, but it is only an illusion. No amount of advancement in science and technology or money can save people from feeling depressed. People get depressed for numerous reasons, which vary from individual to individual, and situations and circumstances. Many times, it is even difficult to determine the exact cause of depression. Even though symptoms of depression vary from person to person, there are some common indicators.

1. **Have You Recently Suffered From Some Unbearable Loss? :** If your answer is yes and your score on the above test is high then the reason may be that your depression is a reaction to some loss in your life. This loss can vary from death of a loved one, if you are married then a divorce or separation from your spouse. Other losses, which may be the reason of your depressed state, may be related with your loosing hope, your self-identity, and faith in yourself or your innocence. You may have lost sight of your self-worth or self-esteem. Any personal loss is surely distressing and a justifiable reason for your depression. What is however not justified is lingering on with such feelings with the passage of time. Time is known to be the greatest healer. You should slowly get yourself together and gather the strength to face what lies ahead of you rather than brood over what was. Do not loose hope because hope is the vessel, which ferries one through turbulent waters. Remember that it is with hope great missions have been accomplished. So go ahead and change your outlook from hopelessness to hopefulness.
2. **Your Suppressed Anger Can Be The Cause of Your Depression:** You may be the kind who swallows his rage and does not publicly or openly express it. This gentleman image surely makes you lovable but not without a price which you

have to pay unknowingly. If you are in a habit of suppressing your anger then you are likely to be more susceptible to depression. You may be at peace with others but disturb your own equilibrium. The reason is your unexpressed anger turns inwards and silently takes away your mental peace. To have a mentally healthy life you need to express your emotions as per the demand of the situation. This expression will enable you to give vent to your feelings and make room for fresher ones. Remember stale things always rot and stink – stop stinking!

3. **Chemical Imbalance Can Be A Major Source of Your Depression**: You may be blessed with all that you desired for yet you may be feeling depressed. You have looked all round but have failed to identify any causative factors. If this is the case look within – your brain chemistry may be the source. Get the levels of *noradrenalin*, *serotonin*, and *dopamine* tested. Medical science has established the relationship between the levels of these chemicals present in your brain and susceptibility to depression. These chemicals are involved in the transition of nerve impulses in the brain and are also referred to as *monoamines*. If they are unstable or low then they may be the latent source of your depression. Besides the level of these brain chemicals, many drugs and alcohol are also known to bring about physiological changes within you disturbing the state of equilibrium within you. Your depression may also be the resultant of such changes – check your drug and alcohol usages.

4. **Look Up Your Family History – Your Depression May Be Genetic**: Studies have shown that many people who suffer from depression have a family history of the same. This is so because genetic vulnerabilities cause depression – it is in your genes to be susceptible to depression. Your genes cannot be tampered with but you surely can learn to cope better with stressful and challenging situations and conquer over your vulnerable inheritance.

5. **Stress May Be The Reason of Your Distress**: Life would be simple indeed, if our biological and psychological needs were

automatically gratified. However, there are many obstacles, both environmental and personal, that interfere. Such obstacles place adjustive demands or stress on us and disturb our state of equilibrium. We have all passed through many stressful situations. They make us unhappy because we fail to cope effectively with them. This failure in turn makes us devalue ourselves and we become depressed. Do not worry if stress is one of the causes of your depression. Handle your stressful situation with a positive attitude. To make this positive attitude a way of your life it has to become a part of your thought, plan, and action and must be practised continuously. Thus, if you want to be stress free you must have a positive attitude. You must approach life's stressful situations with a positive pattern of thought. This positive thinking on your part will surely do wonders for your level of stress and thereby directly dip your depression level.

6. **Perfection Many A Times Leads To Depression – Do Not Overdo It**: You cannot have everything in perfect order and neither every individual you interact with can be perfect. Many a times, this obsession with perfection becomes a cause of depression since one's expectations become unrealistic which are not met in reality. If your perfectionist nature is causing you problems then it is time to work upon your expectancies, your perception of other people and their work output. Begin looking upon the positive and brighter side. Learn to expect little and appreciate what you receive. Finally remember that nobody is perfect – not even you.

7. **Your Poor Health Might Be The Source of Your Depression**: It is common knowledge that people suffering from terminally ill diseases generally become depressed. They do have valid reasons because they know that their end is near. However, such people should also awaken to the reality that brooding would only shorten their lives all the more. People suffering from heart problems, diabetes, and other diseases also have higher rates of depression. They are depressed because they

are worried about their wellbeing. Worrying will not do any good but adversely affect their health. On the other hand, being happy and having a positive frame of mind will do wonders.

8. **If You Are A Woman, You Are More Prone To Depression**: It is a scientifically established fact that women are more prone to depression. As compared to men, they are almost twice as likely to experience depression. The major reason for this is the high frequency of hormonal changes within them – attaining puberty, menstruation, pregnancy and childbirth and finally menopause.

9. **Continued Exposure To Violence or Fear of It Makes Women More Susceptible To Depression:** Apart from physical causes, there are several psychosocial reasons for the high rate of depression in women. Studies have shown that women are exposed more to violence then men – the environment at home, at work or even on the streets may be hostile and result in feelings of insecurity or loss of self - confidence leading to depression. Many times because of such factors, depression in women becomes a learned response. This response, with the passage of time, becomes hard to unlearn and depression becomes a permanent trait.

10. **Childhood Abuse Also Leaves A Permanent Imprint Leading To Depression:** The fairer sex is generally thought to be the weaker one and thus subjugated to abuse from a very tender age. This childhood abuse can be of many types ranging from sexual abuse, neglect, physical abuse and emotional abuse. Whatever is the type of abuse, depending upon its duration and intensity, it can trigger depression in women either in childhood or in adulthood.

11. **Stressful Events Can Trigger Depression In Women:** Depression in women can be caused by divorce, death, job loss, or illness. Any stressful event, especially if it is not dealt with properly, can trigger depression in women.

TAMING THE DEVIL OF DEPRESSION

Dealing with depression is different for everyone. There is no such specific remedy which works like a magic wand and applicable for curing depression. This is so because the causes of depression are far and wide and different people react differently towards these causes. What may depress one may not affect another. In addition, there are individual differences in the exhibition of signs of depression – they vary from individual to individual. In short, the causes and signs of depression are dependent upon ones personality and his surrounding environment.

However, there surely are some psychological tips, which can help prevent one going into a state of depression as well as overcoming it. Remember that the most effective treatment depends on the personality, experiences, and coping styles of person who has depression.

1. **Talk To Your Family Doctor or A Clinical Psychologist/ Counselor**: Since different causes of depression can cause different signs of depression, they require different types of treatment. This treatment may require taking a combination of antidepressants, talk therapy, cognitive behavioural therapy, and lifestyle changes. The first step should be to get in touch with your family doctor or clinical psychologist/counselor. It is always good to reach out for help, being honest and accepting that you have a psychological problem, which requires medical attention.
2. **Get Rest, Eat Right, And Get Exercise**: This is one piece of advice, which anyone and everyone gives for any ailment – physical or mental. You yourself are aware of the fact that a healthy mind stays only in a healthy body. Erratic lifestyle can cause stress leading to other health problems. These individually or collectively will end up making you depressed. Yoga can be very beneficial and so can a simple morning walk. Your diet also needs to be restricted, controlled, and balanced. All these together will help elevate your spirits.
3. **Give Yourself A Break-And Permission To Say No**: If you are in a habit of setting irrationally high standards then its time to let go of them – just chill. Setting high standards and

achieving the targets will create anxiety leading to stress and thereby depression. Plan things in a phased manner and go about achieving your goals step by step without creating unreasonable pressure upon yourself. Take breaks and enjoy vacations. Most important learn to say no to your excessive demands as well as those from others. In short, prioritize your lifestyle for healthy living.

4. **Reach Out To The World Around You**: Come out of your cocoon and look at the world around you. It can impart more wisdom to you than all the sages can. Share some moments with the underprivileged, helping them in whatever way possible and experience the joys of sharing. If you own a garden, spend some time gardening and connect with nature. Take a stroll in the park and listen to the chirping of birds. In nature, you will find infinite places of joy, but to experience this you need to give your valuable time. You can also spend your spare time constructively being involved in religious activities. Visit your holy shrine and experience the peace interacting with your creator.
5. **Express Yourself**: Expression of feelings is the key to a good mental health. Feelings are never wrong. They are the reflection of your honesty within. Bottled up feelings weigh you down and we start behaving in unnatural ways. So give vent to your feelings taking the situation and circumstances into consideration. It is always good to express ourselves as it gives us more space within for generation of fresh and healthy feelings.
6. **Alter Your Perception**: Much of human psychological problems are there because inherently we focus much on the negative side of events. This action of our conditions our thought patterns and our brain thus trained to look and evaluate the darker side of things. We need to shift of focus of attention and remember that there is a positive side also to every negative event in our life. Mathematically even two negatives make up a positive. So train yourself to look at the

positive side of things as well. This will condition your brain and a balance will be struck in your mood enabling you to overcome depression.

7. **Learn To Be Appreciative**: Count your blessings and name them one by one and it will surprise you what has been done for you by others. Mostly we have a tendency to think and list things that others have not done for us. We surely have expectations from others to fulfill our needs but it is not possible for the other to fulfil every need of ours. We have to place ourselves in their place and then think if it was possible. Children often make unnecessary demands from parents but parents do not always do the needful. It is never that parents do not love their children but they use their discretion as well as act within their limitations. In the same way when our demands are not met, we should not have a grudge. In fact, we should be grateful and thankful for what all has so far been done for us and will be done in the near future. Thus, we have to develop an attitude of gratitude. This gratitude will make us feel appreciative, giving us positive vibes, leading to feelings of contentment and happiness. Cribbing on the other hand will only lead us into depression. Learn to appreciate yourself as well as others in your life.
8. **Extend A Helping Hand**: God helps those who help others. Make this the motto of your life. Helping and sharing can effectively generate feelings of happiness and wellbeing within you. These feelings come to you as a reward. So go out, help others, and chase away your depressive mood.
9. **Accept Reality**: Truth is always stranger than fiction and it cannot be denied. It is and will always remain as truth. We cannot evade it. Denial of reality may give temporary relief but later on, it becomes latent source of our depression. This is not good for our mental health. Unless we accept the truth, we cannot face reality. If we deny it, we cannot evade it for much long. So why go around playing hide and seek. Accept what is there and live with it. Harry Truman has rightly commented,

"*I never give them hell. I just tell the truth, and they think it is hell*". Therefore, let the truth not be hell for you. Let it prevail.

10. **Laughter Is Always The Best Medicine**: A simple smile can do wonders and a wholehearted laugh even more. The smile, the chuckle or the loud laughter are physical expressions of felt happiness. You surely will need a reason to smile or laugh so look around you because you will find many. The comedy shows on television, your own sense of humor, or that of your partner. You can also laugh at yourself thinking of the stupid and funny things you have done. So laugh your depression away.

The psychological tips given may prove useful for avoiding getting depressed or overcoming mild depressive moods. Depression is hard on the person who suffers, and it is tough on the people who love that person. Knowing how to act and what to say can be difficult especially if you do not know the cause of depression. My sincere advice is to find a good psychologist/psychiatrist and get treatment at the earliest.

Chapter 9

The Devil of Phobia's – Scare It

"Almost everyone has an irrational fear or two. Some get nervous at the thought of needles. Others shriek at the sight of a mouse. Still others get dizzy when they look down from tall buildings. For most people, these fears are minor. But for some, these fears are so severe that they cause tremendous anxiety and interfere with normal day-to-day life".

"The greatest danger facing us is ourselves, and irrational fear of the unknown. But there's no such thing as 'the unknown,' only things temporarily hidden, temporarily not understood."

A phobia is a persistent fear of some object or situation that presents no actual danger to the person. The individual realizes that his fears are irrational but from which he cannot free himself. Most of us have minor fears, but in phobic reactions, such fears are intense and interfere with everyday activities. If individuals suffering from phobias attempt to approach rather than avoid the phobic situation, they are overcome by anxiety, which may vary from mild feelings of uneasiness and distress to a full-fledged anxiety attack.

The list of phobias is endless ranging from fear of high places, open places, closed places, blood, being alone, darkness, crowds, contamination or germs fire, and so . All phobias have been given technical names. Some of the common ones are listed in **Table 1** for your knowledge.

PHOBIAS VS NORMAL FEAR

In a dangerous situation, it is normal and even helpful to experience fear. Fear is an adaptive human response and serves as a protection. It activates the automatic "fight-or-fight" response. This makes our body and mind alert and ready for action. We are thus able to respond quickly and protect ourselves.

On the other hand, phobias pose a threat to our wellbeing and disturb our equilibrium making us incapable of an appropriate action.

It is normal for an individual to be afraid of a big bulldog – it looks frightening, but irrational to be afraid of its tiny puppies or any other small breed dog.

EVOLUTION OF PHOBIAS

Phobias have been thought of as attempts to cope with specific internal or external dangers by carefully avoiding the situation likely to bring about whatever is feared. Phobias, thus, are seen as simple defensive reactions in which the person feels he must give in to his fears in order to protect himself. Example: If you are jogging in the park and a snake slithers across the path in front of you, you may quit jogging in that park. However, the anxiety aroused may not simply disappear by your quitting jogging in the park but it may be carried over to any other place you decide to take your jog – outside in a field or even a gymnasium. This in turn may compel you to stop your jogging forever or at least until you are cured of your phobia. In this way, some common phobias and anxieties either grow from a relatively trivial experience or may arise from some horribly frightening experience.

MAIN CAUSES OF PHOBIAS

1. **Direct Experience**: This is when a person develops a phobia after a particularly bad experience. A child that is bitten by a dog may develop a phobia of dogs, or an individual that was trapped in an elevator for hours may develop claustrophobia.
2. **A False Alarm:** This occurs when a person has an unexpected feeling of panic or a panic attack during a certain situation. The individual then associates this alarm response with that particular situation. For example, many people with a phobia of driving haven't been in a car accident, but have experienced a panic attack while driving.
3. **Observing Others**: In some cases it is simply enough to watch or even hear someone else's awful experience. A phobia of doctors can develop after a child hears another child's anguished screams coming from the doctor's office. Phobias

may also develop when children observe the behaviour of a phobic parent.

4. **Being Told:** Sometimes just being warned repeatedly about a certain danger can cause a phobia. A child who has a fretful parent who continually warns of the danger of snakes may develop a phobia of snakes, despite never having seen one in real life.

ARE YOU PHOBIC?

This hypothetical measure will make you aware if any of your common fear has crossed the danger mark and turned into a *common phobia.* Follow the instructions given in the task and respond to the questions asked thereafter.

Task: Sit down in a calm and quite place. Shut your eyes and relax for five minutes. Do not think about anything. After five minutes are over imagine with full intensity your worst fear coming true. For example: getting trapped in a deep pit, all alone in a dark location, standing on top of a very high tower and looking down, asked to give an extempore speech, a spider on your dress, falling into a swimming pool boarding a crowded bus, caught in a storm, trapped inside a very small room, crawling through a tunnel, being marooned on an island, surrounded by fire, chased by a dog, caught in a massive traffic jam, lizard on your bed, snake in your cupboard, cockroach in your handbags, dog pouncing on you so on and so forth. *You also may be experiencing situations in reality, which you fear, then mark your responses based on those situations.*

Immediately after you have gone through this imaginative exercise respond to the following questions with honesty.

1. Did you experience a shortness of breath? Yes/No.
2. Did your heart beat increase? Yes/No.
3. Did you feel unsteady? Yes/No.
4. Did you have feelings of being detached from yourself? Yes/No.
5. Did you experience discomfort in the chest? Yes/No.
6. Did you tremble? Yes/No.
7. Did you feel chocked? Yes/No.

8. Did you sweat? Yes/No.
9. Were you besieged by the fear of going crazy? Yes/No.
10. Did you feel any nausea? Yes/No.
11. Did you experience a fear of imminent death? Yes/No.
12. Did you experience any numbness or tingling sensations? Yes/No.
13. Did you have hot or cold flashes? Yes/No.
14. Did you fear you might faint? Yes/No.
15. Did you experience any unusual sensations in your stomach? Yes/No.

SCORING AND INTERPRETATION

After you have marked, your responses give a point of 1 to every Yes you have ticked. Now total them up. This is your score on this hypothetical measure. If your score lies in the range of 11 – 15 you are *extremely phobic*; 6 - 10 you are *moderately phobic* and if it lies in the range of 0 – 5 you do not appear to be bothered by any phobia presently.

TABLE 1
Some Common Phobias

Acrophobia: Better known as fear of height has caused immense distress to countless people down the years. You feel as if your head is tossing as you look down from great heights during this particular condition of Acrophobia.
Aerophobia: Aerophobia is the other name of fear of flying. Fear of flying is generally developed after an individual watches incidents of plane crashes on the news, suddenly loses a relative or a compeer due to an unfortunate plane crash, or watches movies in which the story centers on a deadly event of an air accident.
Agoraphobia: Agoraphobia involves intense fear and avoidance of any place or situation where escape might be difficult or help unavailable in the event of developing sudden panic-like symptoms.
Arachnophobia: Fear of Spiders. Almost 50 percent of women and 10 percent of men have a fear of spiders.

Brontophobia: Fear of thunderstorms. Brontophobia is also known as Astraphobia, Keraunophobia, Tonitrophobia or the fear of lightning and thunder, especially affects children. However, the symptoms of this specific phobic condition are also quite apparent in adults and teenagers.
Carcinophobia: Extreme fear of cancer. This phobic condition is quite unnatural as it makes the individual afraid of all sorts of negative bodily symptoms. One physical discomfort and the person start believing that he has cancer.
Claustrophobia: Fear of being trapped in small confined spaces. Claustrophobia is a form of anxiety disorder during which a person feels extremely afraid of being in enclosed or confined spaces.
Emetophobia: Fear of vomit. You may be afraid to vomit or you may also feel awkward to see others vomiting.
Monophobia: Fear of being alone. Such people dread to stay alone anywhere.
Mysophobia: Fear of contamination of germs. You may not touch things out of fear of being infected.
Necrophobia: Necrophobia or the fear of the dead is a psychological status when you feel afraid of death or may be you are afraid of dead things.
Ocholophobia: Fear of crowds. Such people avoid going to crowed markets and places.
Pathophobia: Fear of diseases. Such people take extreme measures to avoid being infected.
Pyrophobia: Fear of fire. Such people avoid even lighting a matchstick.
Social Phobia: Social phobia is the fear of being misjudged or the fright of being accused unreasonably. Fear of being evaluated negatively in social situations. Social phobia typically begins in childhood or adolescence.
Zoophobia: Fear of animals in general or particular animal.

IF YOU ARE PHOBIC, FIND HOW IT DEVELOPED

Three major causal patterns have been emphasized in the development of phobias. If you happen to suffer from some common phobia then find how it could have developed.

1. **Your Phobia May Be The Learned Result of Prior Trauma**: If you have a phobia then it may have developed due to a bad experience you have had in the past. If this is the case, you need not be frightened. This type of phobia is not difficult to understand because most of us probably have mild phobias based on previous learning. A person who has been attacked and bitten by dogs may feel uneasy with dogs near him. Phobias can also be the resultant of an all-encompassing pattern of fear and avoidance behaviour. For example, if a child is not left alone to do things on his own level, he in the end, will not have confidence in himself to cope with new situations. He thus learns to avoid the appropriate response where risks or uncertainty is involved.
2. **Your Phobia May Be A Defensive Reaction**: Your phobia may be a defence against threatening impulses. Such phobic reactions may be trying to protect you from situations in which your repressed aggressive or sexual impulses might become dangerous. For example, a husband may develop a phobia of lakes, swimming pools, and other water bodies because on previous occasions he had persistent ideas of drowning his wife. In the same manner, a young mother may develop a phobia of being alone with her unwanted baby, because of recurring fantasies about strangling him.
3. **Your Phobia May Be The Resultant of Displacement of Your Anxiety**: Your phobia may be the resultant of dislocation of your anxiety from a previous situation to the present situation. The situations under which you had experienced stress in the past, through the mechanism of displacement, may have led you to become phobic to formerly innocuous objects. For example, an insecure person who feels that he may be sacked from his job for inefficiency may develop an elevator phobia. Since this person works on the 32nd floor of a high rising building, this phobia makes it impossible for him to get to work. This in turn protects the person from the

possible embarrassment and self-devaluation of being sacked from the job.

Regardless of how one's phobia begins, this behaviour tends to be reinforced by the reduction in anxiety that occurs when the individual avoids the feared situation or stress. Phobias may also be maintained in part by secondary gains, such as increased attention, sympathy, and some control over the behaviour of others. For example, a phobia of driving may enable a housewife to escape from responsibilities outside the home.

OVERCOMING PHOBIAS – BEHAVIOUR THERAPY CAN HELP

You can overcome your phobias because you are aware of the fact that your fear is unreasonable but you cannot do this entirely on your own. You need to visit a psychotherapist who will give you *cognitive behavioural therapy* called *systematic desensitization* or *exposure therapy*. This is a very effective form of therapy as far as phobias are concerned. In order for systematic desensitization to work, it is essential that people be able to identify what they are afraid of. For this reason, the approach has been most successfully applied to phobias and anxieties that can be broken down into basic elements.

Systematic desensitization is based on the principle of *reciprocal inhibition*, in which the person substitutes for the undesired response a response that is incompatible or competitive with it. For example, anxiety responses may be extinguished by gradually associating the anxiety situation or stimulus with a relaxation response.

The first step in systematic desensitization is training in relaxation techniques. This may cover several sessions and homework assignments. The next step involves making up a hierarchy in which various aspects of the anxiety-producing situation are ranked from extremely mild to extremely tense and anxiety filled. The patient is asked to relax and then to experience or imagine each step in the hierarchy, starting at the lower or mild end.

Through repeated short exposures while using the relaxation technique, the person learns to imagine each step without feelings of anxiety. As each step in the hierarchy is "conquered", the person moves on until he or she can experience or imagine the highest level, which used to be the most disturbing, without anxiety. Now comes the final step and that is to carry the learned responses into the actual environment.

SYSTEMATIC DESENSITIZATION IN PRACTICE – TRY IT YOURSELF!

Suppose you are scared of dogs then how are you going to give systematic desensitization to yourself? Follow the simple steps given and they may apply to some other phobias as well.

- **Step 1**: Draw a picture of a dog.
- **Step 2**: Read about dogs.
- **Step 3**: See photographs of dogs.
- **Step 4**: Watch videos or television shows on dogs.
- **Step 5**: Look at dogs from a distance – closely observe them.
- **Step 6**: Repeat the above steps on a regular basis for some days.
- **Step 7**: When you begin to feel a bit comfortable find a puppy and try cuddling it.
- **Step 8**: Give the puppy something to eat.
- **Step 9**: Begin to play with the puppy.
- **Step 10**: Begin to visit a friend who has a grown up but not ferocious dog on a regular basis.
- **Step 11**: Whistle to the dog.
- **Step 12**: When the dog begins to recognize you try patting it in the presence of your friend – it will wag its tail and may try licking your hand showing its affection.
- **Step 13**: Remember a dog is a man's best friend.

TAMING THE DEVIL OF PHOBIAS

If your fears and phobias are not negatively affecting your life and you feel you can do without professional help then here are some tips for you to follow to help you overcome them yourself.

1. **Identify Your Fears**: The first step you should take is to identify your phobia/s and related fears and then note them down.
2. **Make A Hierarchy of Your Fears**: After you have done so arrange your fears related with the phobia in hierarchical order ranging from extremely mild to extremely tense and anxiety filled.
3. **Gain Knowledge About Your Phobia**: The third step is to gain knowledge and understand about your phobia/s and to know how real or irrational they are. This education on your part will play a very decisive role in eradicating or controlling them. You will soon begin to realize that fear is a common emotion in all living organisms. There are many people, who share common fears, and you will not find yourself secluded. Through your educative exercise, you will also realize that you can overcome your fears but only if you want and are determined to do so – where there is a will, there is a way.
4. **Look At Each Situations And Events With A Positive Outlook**: Once you have a good knowledge about your phobia look at the relevant situations and events arousing the fear with a positive outlook. This will help weaken your negative frightful thoughts giving you comfort and confidence. Remember it is all in the mind. Suppose you are afraid of elevators then think about the thousands of people who use it daily in the office buildings, shopping malls, and apartments. Have you ever seen anyone falling from it or dying in it due to suffocation? Inspect an elevator when it is stationary. You will find it well ventilated and equipped with other security features. The positive approach of yours will diminish your fear.
5. **Be Firm**: Once you have made up your mind, to overcome your fears, do not move back. Do not hesitate even if achieving the target looks impossible.
6. **Plan How You Will Approach Your Goal**: You have to make an operational plan which you will put into effect. This plan

should be a gradual one and implimented in steps and stages. Your phobia is not a new fear or a one time fear. It has grown along with you and it will take some time and effort on your part to subdue it.

7. **Think of All Possible Extensions**: Look at your problem from all angles and theoretically prepare yourself on how to overcome them. This will give you a preview of what all you should be prepared for.
8. **Take On The Smaller Portions First**: To begin your actual tasks take up the smaller portions of your phobia first. You should not put yourself at risk by trying to tackle the entire problem in one go. Your discretion should get the better of your valour. For example, if you are afraid of high places do not rush and climb on to the top of a high floor building and try looking down. Take up one floor at a time and look down from there. After a few such attempts, you should begin to feel comfortable. Now it is time that you move to the next floor and so on and so forth.
9. **Relaxation Helps**: If in case you do not succeed in your first attempt just relax. You can do so in many ways. Yoga, meditation, or just take in a deep breathe, hold it for a few seconds, and release it slowly thereafter. You can also begin to count slowly if you come across an anxiety-arousing situation. The time you spend counting will relax your body and calm your nerves. You can also try diverting your attention to some other interesting thing. Get busy socializing and chatting with friends and family.
10. **Put In Regular Efforts:** Confront your phobia on a regular basis. Do not avoid it. Make it a habit to face it until you are victorious.
11. **Reward Yourself With Each Conquest**: When you begin to achieve success in your brave mission, celebrate the occasion. It is time to rejoice and reward your brave efforts.
12.. **You Do Not Loose But Gain**: Once you begin to get success over your mild intensity fears, you will gain courage and

self-confidence to take complete control of the fear arising situation, event or object.

Successful treatment of phobias may lead to a change in your lifestyle. You will gain confidence and your ability to cope with stressful situations will become more powerful. Let not your fears dominate you but have the courage to scare them away.

Chapter 10

The Devil of Sleep Disorders – Lullaby It

"Everyone experiences occasional sleep problems, but getting a good night's sleep is essential for feeling refreshed and alert during the day. Lack of sleep might make you feel foggy and unable to concentrate, or just a lesser version of your normal self. Sleep problems will eventually disrupt your work, family, and personal relationships".

"Early to bed and early to rise makes a man healthy, wealthy, and wise."

An individual spends one third of his lifetime in sleep. Every night one goes to sleep to give rest to his mind and body and save his energies. A good sleep refreshes an individual mentally as well as physically. In simple words, a number of vital tasks are carried out during the period of sleep. These tasks help in maintaining good health and enable people to function at their best. We need sleep to think clearly, react quickly, and create memories. If one does not get adequate sleep, it will have harmful effects on normal functioning.

The amount of sleep needed for daily functioning and physical and mental health varies from individual to individual. Shahrukh Khan, the great actor, once commented in a television program that he sleeps for just four hours. Many other actors, directors, politicians, bureaucrats, industrialists etc., would be doing with less hours of sleep because of their busy schedule. Normally most adults need 7 – 8 of sleep during the night. Small children need to sleep for around 10 – 12 hours and children in preschool and teens require sleep for around 9 hours.

SLEEP AND PERSONALITY TRAITS

How many hours will an individual sleep in a day depends on various factors. Psychologists have classified people into three categories based on amount of sleep they take.

1. The first category is of those who take less sleep. Such people on an average do not require more than 6 hours of sleep in a day. Even with this less amount of sleep, they do not face any type of physical or mental problems and engage in daily

activities in a normal manner. Such types of people tend to be highly ambitious, social and workaholics.

2. The second category is of those who sleep daily for up to 9 hours or more. The excess sleep of theirs does not seem to hamper their physical and mental abilities and neither does it negatively affect their daily working. Such people however have a tendency to feel dejected and are prone to worrying. Most of them are introverts and do not prefer to socialize.
3. The third category is of those who have the normal required sleep of around 7 – 8 hours daily. Most of the population comes under this category and have varying personality traits common with the above categories. Though good and adequate sleep provides for a sound body and mind it is not always necessary that people having normal sleep are normal in all respects. This is so because apart from sleep there are various other psychosocial and economical factors, which affect mental and physical health. Good sleep does enable one to cope better and function efficiently in all types of situations and circumstances by providing the much-needed bodily resource of strength and vigor.

ADVANTAGES OF ADEQUATE SLEEP

1. **Increases Immunity**: During the period of sleep, the body releases various hormones, which are helpful in fighting various types of infections. In this manner, a good night sleep keeps you away from possible ailments and helps you recover from those you are presently suffering from.
2. **It Keeps You Safe From Many Ailments**: Research has shown that people who sleep well and adequately suffer less from problems of high blood pressure, heart diseases, and other medical conditions.
3. **It Contributes To Healthy Growth**: Adequate sleep is very important for children as much of their early growth and development depends upon it. Many hormones produced and released during the period of deep sleep are essential for proper growth. They help in building muscle mass and repair cells and tissues in both children as well as adults.

4. **It Re-energizes You**: Sleep also helps in determining how your body will use its energy. People who sleep well are recharged with required energy for proper functioning. Their bodies require lesser calorie and carbohydrate intakes. They are active and physically fit. On the other hand, people, who sleep less, generally tend to be overweight and have a high probability of becoming diabetic. They have low energy levels and require consuming food with high calories and carbohydrates.
5. **It Refreshes Your Mood**: A sound sleep positively affects your mood. You tend to be easygoing, cheerful, behave in a normal manner, and handle inter-personal relationships lovingly. On the other hand, people who sleep less, easily get irritated, exhibit abnormal behaviour, and have trouble with relationships. Their less sleep can also at times, lead them into a depressive mood.

EFFECTS OF SLEEP DEPRIVATION

What will happen if one is deprived of sleep for many days at a stretch? The individual will become irritable or aggressive. He will also show a decline in his power to concentrate. After 4 – 5 days of sleeplessness, he will experience bouts of sleep, have illusions, and not feel like doing any work. There is also a probability that he may have delusions – hear voices, which are non-existence. He may also hallucinate – see things, which do not exist. Both these if present are reflective of his unhealthy mental state and symptoms of mental ailments. This ailment is technically known as bipolar mood disorder and is the result of inadequate sleep.

HOW WELL DO YOU SLEEP?

Take the following test, which helps you; know how well you sleep during the night. Read each statement carefully and then assign the "point" (0-3) in the blank space provided at the beginning of each statement. *The point you choose to assign is to be based on the frequency of occurrences with regards to the statement in the past two or three months.*

POINTS

0 – Never.

1 – Sometimes.

2 – Most of the time.

3 – Always.

_____1. You take more than thirty minutes each night to fall asleep.

_____2. You consistently awaken several times each night and then have trouble falling back to sleep.

_____3. You consistently awaken too early in the morning, much before your scheduled time.

_____4. You often feel sleepy during the day.

_____5. You take frequent naps.

_____6. You fall asleep at inappropriate times during the day.

_____7. People sleeping next to you complain that you snore loudly during the night.

_____8. People sleeping next to you complain that you snort during the night.

_____9. People sleeping next to you complain that you make choking sounds during the night.

_____10. People sleeping next to you complain that you stop breathing for short periods during the night.

_____11. You have creeping, tingling, or crawling feelings in your legs or arms that are relieved by moving or massaging them, especially in the evening and when trying to fall asleep.

_____12. People sleeping next to you have told you that during sleep you jerk your legs and arms.

_____13. You have vivid, dreamlike experiences while falling asleep or dozing.

_____14. You have episodes of sudden muscle weakness when you are angry or fearful, or when you laugh.

_____15. You feel as though you cannot move when you first wake up.

______16. You have difficulty staying awake when sitting still, watching television or reading.
______17. You have difficulty concentrating.
______18. You feel irritable for no genuine reasons.
______19. Others tell you that you are looking tired.
______20. You react very slowly.
______21. You have emotional outbursts.
______22. Require tea or coffee to keep you going.
______ **Total**

SCORING AND INTERPRETATION

After having assigned the points, total them up. This total is your score on this measure. If you have scored in the range of 50 - 66, you have *extremely high sleep disturbances*; in the range of 34 – 49, you have *high sleep disturbances;* in the range of 17 – 33 *moderate sleep disturbances* and in the range of 0 – 16 do not seem to have sleep disturbances presently.

COMMON SLEEP DISORDERS – FIND YOURS IF YOU HAVE ONE

Though there are approximately seventeen types of common sleep disorders listed, you need to be aware about only a few of them since most of the individuals suffer from either one of them. The rest of them are summarized under other common sleep disorders.

1. **Insomnia**: Many people lie down in their beds at night and try hard falling asleep but they fail to do so. Such people if they do manage to go off to sleep have trouble maintaining it. Most of us have experienced this problem sometime or the other. This problem is the result of various factors which include stress, change in time due to travel across different time zones, change in sleeping schedule, a nap in the noontime, consuming stimulants like caffeine and nicotine, etc. If this insomnia is short lived, there is nothing to worry but if it persists then it is sounding an alarm, warning you about the advent of a sleep disorder. It is time then to identify the causes of your insomnia and take appropriate action.

2. **Delayed Sleep Phase Syndrome**: The delayed sleep phase syndrome is one of the most common complications of sleep-wake patterns. Patients with this syndrome are able to get plentiful sleep; it just differs from traditional sleep-wake patterns. This syndrome results when a persons internal biological clock does not match his or her external environment. This should not be confused with a jetlag because it is not activated by travel or a change in external environment. Rather, the patient's propensity to fall asleep is simply "delayed" in relation to other people's. Subsequently, a patient with this syndrome is desynchronized with the routine that governs most of his or her life. People suffering from this syndrome are unable to fall asleep before 2 a.m. and have extreme difficulty waking early in the morning, which disturbs their daily scheduled activities – school, work etc.
3. **Hypopnea Syndrome**: This is a condition when an individual experiences abnormally shallow breathing or slow respiratory rate while sleeping. This should not be confused with *sleep apnea* as some air is being passed through the mouth or nose. This disorder leads to the rising of level of blood due to decrease in oxygen intake and its level is proportinate to the degree of obstruction. Hypopnea interrupts sleep patterns and results in the individual feeling fatigued, inability to concentrate, irritability, and headaches. They get extremely tired because they cannot sleep. This constant sleepiness is the biggest symptom for the individual. Other symptoms include severe snoring including intermittent bouts of choking noises or very loud snores that have a long silence afterwards. Along with this there is also a feeling of depression, becoming forgetful, experiencing personality changes such as moodiness, inability of concentrate, feeling lethargic, anxiety, and morning headaches. The syndrome negatively affects a person's quality of life. The excessive sleepiness can cause car accidents, inability to concentrate and reduced productivity. It can also lead to emotional problems and a lesser quality of relationships. Hypopnea, that is not severe, can be treated

by the patient losing weight or by not sleeping on his or her back. Quitting smoking, not drinking alcohol, and not using sedatives before bed can also be a useful treatment for this disorder. Physical exercise that also strengthens respiratory muscles can also be quite effective. Severe hypopnea on the other hand requires surgery.

4. **Sleep Apnea**: An interruption in breathing occurs during sleep for approximately more than ten seconds in this condition. This disorder is very common and can be very serious and life threatening. The most common type of sleep apnea is *obstructive sleep apnea.* During an episode of obstructive sleep apnea, the effort to inhale air creates a suction that collapses the windpipe. Airflow may be blocked for a period of 10 – 60 seconds while the individual, in sleep, struggles to breath. When this blockage occurs the oxygen levels in the blood drop and the brain immediately responds by waking the individual thus enabling him to tighten the airway muscles and open the windpipe. The individual may snort or gasp, then go back to snoring. This entire episode can occur hundred times in one night. Upon finally waking up in the morning such individuals always feel sleepy and may even experience personality changes, such as irritability or depression. The effects of sleep apnea can also lead to morning headaches, loss of interest in sex, decline in mental functioning, high blood pressure, irregular heartbeats, and an increased risk of heart attacks or strokes. The causes of sleep apnea are generally physical in nature, including excess weight or tissue, large tonsils or adenoids, nasal congestion or blocking or a unique shaped head, neck or chin. Treatment includes a combination of behavioural changes, ventilation assistance, drug therapy, and surgery, which allows most people with sleep apnea to be treated successfully, although it may take some time to determine the most effective and least intrusive treatment. Polysomnography testing is usually required after beginning a treatment to determine how effective it has been.

5. **Narcolepsy**: This is characterized by excessive daytime sleepiness, which often culminates in falling asleep spontaneously, but unwillingly at inappropriate occasions. Such people have sleep attacks during the day even if they have had a normal sleep at night. It is assumed that this sleep disorder is due to the brain's inability to regulate sleep-wake cycles normally. Narcolepsy may also be genetic but it also seems to be influenced by environmental factors. It can also be the result of brain damage from a head injury or any neurological disease. The effects of this disorder can be dangerous because such individuals tend to fall asleep even while performing critical tasks like driving or handling machines, which requires alertness and attentiveness. People with narcolepsy may also experience a loss of muscle control during emotional situations; have hallucinations, disrupted nighttime sleep, and temporary paralysis when they wake up. Treatment for narcolepsy includes stimulants and prescribed antidepressants. Taking short voluntary naps during the daytime can also be helpful.
6. **Snoring**: Snoring is one of the most common, mildest and irritating of all the disorders especially for others sleeping next to the snorer. This disorder many a times is confused with sleep apnea because of the snore, which in itself is not a permanent feature of sleep apnea. Snoring occurs when a narrow airway gets in the way of smooth breathing and creates the snoring sound. This narrowing happens because of either a poor sleeping posture, excessive body weight or some physical abnormalities of the throat. However, when one is snoring it is not necessary that there is an obstruction in the airway as in the case of sleep apnea. Remedies for controlling snoring are many – sleeping on your side, elevating the head of your bed, or loosing some excess weight.
7. **Restless Leg Syndrome**: This is characterized by an irrespirable urge to move legs. This urge is the resultant of either feeling uncomfortable while lying down, tingly, or creeping sensations in the legs or effected limbs. The

movement eases these feelings but only for sometime. People suffering from this syndrome often also have *periodic limb movement disorder*, which is characterized by a sudden involuntary movement of the arms and/or legs during sleep – kicking the legs. Severe restless leg syndrome is most common in elderly people, though symptoms can develop at any age. In some cases, restless leg syndrome may be linked to conditions such as anemia, pregnancy, or diabetes. Treatment includes alternative therapies, lifestyle changes, and even nutritional supplements. Some prescribed drug therapies are also available.

8. **Other Common Sleep Disorders**: Other common sleep disorders are *Bruxism*: This is characterized by involuntary grinding or clenching of the teeth while sleeping. *Cataplexy*: Characterized by a sudden weakness in the motor muscles that can result in collapse to the floor. *Night terror*: Technically called *Pavor nocturnes*, is characterized by an abrupt awakening from sleep with behaviour consistent with terror. *Parasomnias*: This is characterized by disruptive sleep-related events involving inappropriate actions during sleep stages like sleepwalking and night terrors. *Rapid eye movement disorder*: This is characterized by the acting out of violent or dramatic dreams while in the period of rapid eye movement sleep. *Sleep paralysis*: Often seen as a part of *narcolepsy*, this is characterized by temporary paralysis of the body shortly before or after sleep. It may be accompanied by visual, auditory, or tactile hallucinations. This is not considered a disorder unless it is severs. *Sleepwalking* or *somnambulism*: This is characterized by engaging in activities that are normally associated with wakefulness, which may include walking, without the conscious knowledge of the person. *Nocturia*: This is characterized by a frequent need to get up and go to the bathroom to urinate in the night. It differs from *enuresis*, or bed-wetting, in which the person does not arouse from sleep, but the bladder nevertheless empties. *Somniphobia*: This is a phobia, which is associated with going to sleep and a disorder on both counts.

TAMING THE DEVIL OF SLEEP DISORDERS

1. **Follow A Strict Sleep Schedule**: It is best to follow a definite schedule for going to sleep and waking up in the morning. The best schedule is the golden saying of early to be and early to rise. You should stick to this schedule even on weekends and holidays or else it will disturb your body clock. Remember if you get up in the morning when the sun has not dawned then light your room brightly – it will drive away your sleepiness and make you active.
2. **Exercise In The Evening**: Playing outdoor games in the evening time or doing exercises have many benefits. It tones up your physical and mental systems by reducing your stress and anxieties, builds up your appetite and brings in an appropriate level of fatigue to put you to sleep once you lie down on the bed at night.
3. **Control Your Diet Intake**: Avoid having fatty rich food since they take a lot of time to digest which will involuntarily keep you awake. Consuming spicy and acidic food during the evening can also cause trouble in your stomach and lead to heartburns, which worsen when one lies down hence avoid them. Do not take in much liquid before bedtime or else you will end up frequenting the toilets for urination.
4. **Take A Light Meal At Night**: Though taking a walk after your diner is useful but if you have stuffed yourself, the total time for digestion also goes up. Heavy eating can make you feel uncomfortable in the night and disturb your sleep.
5. **Say No To Caffeine And Nicotine Before Bedtime**: Many people are in a habit of having tea, coffee or smoking after dinner. Tea, coffee, and colas, contain caffeine and cigarettes, which contain nicotine, are stimulants that drive your sleep away. Their effects can last up to 8 hours and you are forced to stay awake.
6. **Take A Walk After Dinner**: Taking a walk after dinner helps in the quick digestion of the dinner you have had. Sleeping right away after dinner may cause you uneasiness in the stomach and thereby disturb your sleep.

7. **Avoid Taking Alcoholic Drinks Before Bedtime**: Generally, people have the notion that a small peg of an alcoholic drink before bedtime acts as a tranquilizer and is thus harmless. It surely puts you to sleep very soon but it keeps you only in the lighter stages of sleep. You will end up waking up in the middle of the night when the tranquilizing effect has worn off.
8. **Avoid Taking Naps In The Afternoon**: Naps in the noontime do help boost your brainpower but they can also make your sleep difficult at nighttime. Avoid naps in the noontime if you find them interfering with your night sleep. Even if you do take a nap in the noontime, do so before 2 p.m. and keep then short. A half hour to forty-five minutes nap is sufficient to energize and refresh you.
9. **Relax Before Going To Bed**: After you have taken your walk, spend some time in relaxing by watching television, reading, listening to music, meditating, or praying. This will relax you and help take your mind of the problems you had to tackle throughout the day or the ones that are still there to tackle the next day.
10. **Do Not Lie In Bed If You Cannot Sleep**: Just lying in bed trying to put yourself to sleep will make you all the more restless. In such a case, it is best to engage yourself in some light activity like reading or watching television. Do not leave your mind ideal or else it will become a devils workshop.
11. **Make Your Bedroom Sleep Friendly**: A bedroom is for resting and sleeping so accordingly set its interiors. Your bedroom should be well ventilated and have a bed of an appropriate size. Do not have things in it that may distract your attention – such as electronic gadgets making noise, bright lights, television, or computers. Your bed should be cozy and comfortable and the bedding suitable for the climate. In summers, try keeping appropriate temperatures of your air-conditioning in which you feel comfortable. It should not be too cold.
12. **Expose Yourself To Adequate Amount of Sunlight In The Daytime**: The sun light is the source of all life on earth and

without which there will be no existence. Apart from other things, it is also the key to regulating our daily sleep patterns. Try to catch some of the beneficial rays of the sun daily for around thirty minutes each day. You will also end up getting vitamin D as a bonus.

13. **Seek Medical Help If You Keep Having Sleep Problems**: Though sleeplessness cannot be cured by medicines but they do assist you in having your share of sleep. However, if you take sleeping pills on a regular basis you body gets immune and you have to shift to higher doses. A doctor can only help if there is a physiological problem like obstruction in the airway.

The best doctor for your sleep disorder is you because in most of the cases it is self-created. The best medicine thus is to lullaby your worries, stresses, anxieties, and tensions for the night and recharge your energies with good sleep to take them on the next day. It is truly said that a good start is half the battle won. So make a promise to yourself and do not quit until you comfortably rest through the night. Good night and sleep well.

Chapter 11

The Devil of Suspiciousness – Teach It Trust

"Suspicion is far more to be wrong than right; more often unjust than just. It is no friend to virtue, and always an enemy to happiness. There is nothing makes a man suspect much, more than to know little, and therefore men should remedy suspicion by procuring to know more, and not keep their suspicions in smother".

"Suspicion is a mental picture seen through an imaginary keyhole"

This is a type of a psychological condition, which is associated with and related to many other disorders. People suffering from it have long-term, widespread, and unwarranted suspicions that other people are hostile, threatening, or degrading. They have no supporting evidence for this paranoid behaviour of theirs hence it is considered as abnormal. It is very difficult to get along with such people since their quarrelsome and doubting nature often elicits hostility in others. In the course of time, people begin to avoid them and this reinforces in them their pessimistic beliefs. They are also known to promptly challenge the loyalty of friends and loved ones and tend to carry long grudges. In short their suspicion is far more wrong than right and more often unjust than just. It is no friend to their virtue, and always an enemy to their happiness and those of others associated with them.

HOW SUSPICIOUS ARE YOU?

To be suspicious is human nature and all of us have our share of suspicions related with various things and peoples. Our suspicious nature is normal as long as the same does not begin to dominate and govern our thoughts and life. The line of demarcation is thin and a matter of degrees since we never know when an unrealistic thought will take control of our minds. This measure will assess your typical belief patterns and through it determine the presence or absence of the devil of suspicion within you.

Read each statement carefully and then assign the "point" (0-3) in the blank space provided at the beginning of each statement. *The point you choose to assign is to be based on the frequency with which you display the characteristic traits in the given statement.*

POINTS

0 – Never.
1 – Sometimes.
2 – Most of the time.
3 – Always.

_____ 1. I feel that I cannot put trust on other people.
_____ 2. I feel that other people have hidden motives.
_____ 3. I feel that others will try to use me if I am not watchful.
_____ 4. I feel that I have to be on guard at all times.
_____ 5. I feel that it is not safe to confide in other people.
_____ 6. I feel that people who act friendly towards me are trying to use or exploit me.
_____ 7. I feel that people will take advantage of me if I give them a chance.
_____ 8. I feel that, for the most part, other people are unfriendly.
_____ 9. I feel that other people will deliberately try to humiliate me.
_____ 10. I feel that other people deliberately want to annoy me.
_____ 11. I feel that I will be in serious trouble if I let other people think they can get away by mistreating me.
_____ 12. I feel that if other people find out things about me, they will use them against me.
_____ 13. I feel that people often say one thing and mean something else.
_____ 14. I feel that a person whom I am close to could be disloyal or unfaithful.
_____ **Total Score**

SCORING AND INTERPRETATION

After having assigned the points total them us. This total will be your score on this measure. If you have scored in the range of 32 - 42, you have an *extremely high suspicious nature*. If your score is in the range of 22 – 31, you have a *highly suspicious nature*; if it is in the range of 11 – 21, you have a *moderately suspicious nature* and if it is in the range of 0 – 10 you are *not suspicious* by nature.

ASSOCIATED DISORDERS AND CAUSES – BEWARE IF YOU ARE HIGHLY SUSPICIOUS

Suspicious people can be classified broadly into two types. First are those who have their doubts and suspicions but can be convinced to overcome the same based on facts. The second category consists of people who have irrational and irrelevant doubts and suspicions and no amount of evidence can make them go against their convictions. The people falling in the second category may be suffering from or susceptible to disorders such as paranoid personality, psychosis, schizophrenia, mania etc.

1. **Paranoid Personality Disorder**: This is a type of personality disorder in which, an individual becomes suspicious by temperament. However, this disorder can be overcome through the process of healthy communication. (*This disorder is discussed in detail in the chapter on Personality Dis*orders).
2. **Schizophrenia**: This is a very serious psychological disorder and individuals suffering from it develop a very high level of suspiciousness, which is very difficult to eradicate. They feel that other people are plotting and planning against them and adopting various methods to eliminate them. This suspiciousness along with other predominant symptoms makes their life miserable.
3. **Delusional Disorder**: People suffering from this disorder harbour some specific types of permanent doubts in their mind. If these are not corrected and altered, they remain with the person throughout his life. Such people though carry on with their daily routine in a normal manner but harbour irrational doubts related with those around them. This leads to them becoming socially isolate and not liked by many people.
4. **Alcoholism And Other Substance Abuse or Dependence**: People who have been consuming alcohol or other drugs, for an extended period are prone to become suspicious because of increased imaginative prowess, which largely is delusional and hallucinatory.
5. **Psychosis**: Sudden and unexpected untoward incidences such of death of a loved one, loss in business, loss of job,

theft, public insult etc. can lead to the development of acute psychosis. People suffering from this type of disorder also tend to become suspicious by nature.

6. **Other Associated Mental Disorders**: People suffering from disorders such as mania, depression dementia, obsessive - compulsive disorder, agoraphobia etc., also tend to develop a tendency of suspiciousness.
7. **Physical Ailments**: People suffering from ailments such as AIDS, cancer, fits, etc., also tend to become suspicious by nature.
8. **Consumption of Prescribed Medicines**: Some medicines, such as steroids, thyroxin, etc., which are being consumed by patients, for the treatment of other ailments may give rise to suspiciousness. However, this is not true with every individual and with those whom it is true their suspiciousness decreases once they have taken their course of the medicines.
9. **Other Causes**: Suspiciousness can also be the resultant of a threatening domestic atmosphere experienced during childhood. Such an atmosphere leads to the generation of profound insecurities contributing towards development of a doubtful and suspicious temperament.

TAMING THE DEVIL OF SUSPICIOUSNESS

Suspicious nature cannot be cured on its own and there are as such no self-help remedies – it is rightly said in Hindi – there is no treatment for suspiciousness (*Shak ka koi ilaj nahi hai*). Treatment has to be carried on by either a psychiatrist or a clinical psychologist/counselor who will help identify the exact underlying cause of the individual's suspiciousness and give required therapy/medication.

However, if one wants to help someone who is suspicious he can try following the advice given here. For treatment to be effective, it is essential that an individual who is suspicious by temperament must realize this fact and accept the same. This is an uphill task because such individuals find it difficult to put trust on others. Once this acceptance is established the following procedure can be adopted in order as listed:

1. Prepare a list of all the suspicions.
2. Segregate the strong ones and minor ones.
3. First, take up the minor ones and try talking them out with supportive evidence. Observe the results your efforts have brought about. If you have succeeded then try instilling some more faith into the person.
4. Wait for some days before you take up another issue. Carry on with a trust-building exercise.
5. Repeat steps 3 – 4 for each issue taken up and then move ahead.
6. Now move on to the next level—the stronger ones. Be prepared it is going to be an uphill task and time consuming. Have patience and do not hurry. Keep on with the trust instilling exercise. The person should keep trust in you.
7. Talk with the individual and try finding the root cause of his suspicions. You will have to dig deep into his past.
8. If you find the reasons of his suspicious nature embedded in some past happenings, try unfurling the jumbled mysteries. Generally, such people do not openly discuss their reasons for their deep-rooted suspicions but keep them bottled up within themselves. Once it is in the open, then the issues can be amicably sorted and suspicion turned into trust.

IMPORTANT ADVICE

1. Remember that every person has some amount of suspicious tendency within him – it is human nature. Treatment for suspicion only becomes essential when it goes beyond limits and starts to adversely affect interpersonal relationships creating disturbances and discord.
2. The family members of the person who is highly suspicious should take care not to offend or emotionally arouse him in a negative manner. This will instigate him and make things worse for all.
3. If a person's suspicion has crossed normal limits, the family members must seek immediate medical attention. Prolonged suspicion can lead to the commitment of heinous crimes.

4. Suspicion may be the outcome of various underlying reasons and only a psychiatrist/clinical psychologist/counselor can identify the same and provide professional help.

If you are suspicious by temperament, you should resolve the same by procuring to know more, and not keep them in smother. As human beings, we all want to be happy and free from misery. We all are aware that the key to happiness is inner peace but the greatest obstacles to our inner peace are disturbing emotions such as anger, attachment, fear, and suspicion. We have to learn first to keep ourselves in peace and then only we can keep peace with others. He who dwells in peace is suspicious of none, but he who is discontented and restless is tossed with many suspicions, and is neither quiet himself nor lets others to be quiet.

Chapter 12

The Devil of Irritability – Defuse It

"Irritability is a state of extreme sensitivity to stimulation of any kind. Very often, these people feel stressed, impatient or might easily become angry. It is the early sign of overwork and strain. It can also be the result of crisis in a relationship or fear of failure and family problems. It is a kind of signal, that an unpleasant or potentially threatening situation cannot be avoided or solved in an appropriate way. Psychological causes of irritability can include mild forms of adjustment problems or stress as well as more severe psychiatric problems or disorders".

> "Irritating people cannot live without irritating. That is their life and they must have their daily quota, and if you get irritated, you add fuel to a fire."

There hardly must be any individual, at least in this universe, who has not expressed his irritation over some issue or the other. Many times, we get angry over small issues and expressing the same show our irritation. This expressed irritation can be in the form of a physical attack, use of abusive language, or just through gestures. This expression of our irritation is a psychological condition, which is the resultant of frustration. When our needs are thwarted and we cannot achieve our goals, we get frustrated. This frustration leads us to become irritated, which is then expressed through aggressive acts. The intensity of expressed irritation does vary from individual to individual and depends on various other situations and circumstances. If in due course of time, an individual cannot get control over the causes of his frustrations, his level of tolerance goes down, and he begins to react in an irritated manner to even minor issues. This type of irritable behaviour does a lot of damage to the individual especially in the management of healthy interpersonal relationships. If ones irritable behaviour persists for a long time it can lead to neurasthenia, depression, anxiety, mania, schizophrenia, and personality disorders.

TEST YOUR IRRITABILITY – THE IRRITABILITY QUOTIENT

The following measure will help you determine your level of irritability. Read each statement carefully and then assign the "*reaction point*" (0 -

4) in the blank space provided at the beginning of each statement. *The "reaction point" you have to assign are to be based on either one of these following reactions you will have towards the event in the statement*:

REACTION POINT

0 - You will feel very little or no annoyance.
1 - You will feel a little irritated.
2 - You will feel moderately upset.
3 - You will feel quite angry.
4 - You will feel very angry.

_____ 1. You come home after purchasing a new appliance and plugging it in you find it does not work.

_____ 2. You get an electrician to fix up your home electricity on an urgent basis and he overcharges you.

_____ 3. You are reprimanded for committing errors while those done by your colleagues are overlooked.

_____ 4. While driving your car you get stuck in the mucky roadside.

_____ 5. You address your conversation to someone and he does not respond.

_____ 6. When people make tall and false claims about themselves.

_____ 7. When someone accidentally bumps into you and spills the tea, you are carrying on your clothes.

_____ 8. You have organized the files on your worktable and someone searching for a file disturbs them.

_____ 9. You are visiting a historical monument and the local tourist guides begin to relentlessly pester you for hiring them.

_____ 10. You are going on a planned vacation with friends but they back out at the last moment thus forcing you to cancel the trip.

_____ 11. When people make you the butt of their jokes.

_____ 12. Your car is caught in a traffic jam and the driver of the car behind you is constantly blowing his horn.

_____ 13. You left your car parked in a wrong position, obstructing the gateway of other cars, and upon returning the parking attendant remarks upon your inconsiderate thought.

_____ 14. You are blamed for a mistake made by someone else.

_____ 15. You are busy doing some mathematical calculations and your spouse/friend is constantly humming a song.

_____ 16. Your neighbour forgets to return a screwdriver he had borrowed a few days back from you.

_____ 17. You did not get time to do an advance booking for a movie ticket and on returning home your family members constantly begin to nag you upon your forgetfulness.

_____ 18. If you are discussing on some important matter with your spouse or partner and he/she is not giving you a fair chance to express your opinion.

_____ 19. If a person, with a shallow knowledge or no knowledge on a topic you are well versed with, begins to argue with you on the same.

_____ 20. If someone pokes his nose into a heated discussion, you are having with another person.

_____ 21. If you are getting late for an urgent meeting and the car ahead of you is not giving you way to overtake.

_____ 22. If you step over a banana peel thrown on the footpath by some ill-mannered person and just miss slipping down.

_____ 23. If unknown people, begin to mock upon your attire.

_____ 24. While running down the stairs in a hurry your shirt sleeves get caught on the sharp edge of the banister and get torn.

_____ 25. You are making a call from a public telephone booth but it fails to connect you despite your putting in only coin you have.

_____ **Total**

SCORING AND INTERPRETATION

After having assigned your "*reaction point*" to the statements, total them up. This total will be your Irritability Quotient. You can now interpret your total score according to the score you have obtained on this measure as follows:

0 - 45: If you have scored in this range you are unique since rarely anyone will get this score. Your score indicates that you experience an exceptionally low amount of anger and annoyance. Hats off to you cool fellow – others may get irritated by your coolness!!

46 - 55: This range indicates that as compared with the average population you are substantially more peaceful.

56 - 75: This range of scores is the average one. Most of the population falls in this category. This score range indicates that you respond to life's annoyances with an average amount of anger.

76 - 85: This score range is an above average one. It indicates that you are substantially more irritable than the average person. You have frequent outbursts of anger and tend to get irritated easily with many of life's daily annoyances.

86 - 100: Only a few percent of the adult population fall in this category. This score range is an indication that you are abnormal, having excessive excitability, which easily triggers your anger leading to show your annoyance or impatience all the time and everywhere. The irritability of yours does not diffuse easily and you harbor negative feelings even long after the initiating event. You may not be liked by people and having very few true friends who somehow tolerate you. You may also be suffering from frequent headaches, high blood pressure, and neurasthenia apart from other psychological disorders. You also exhibit a tendency towards impulsiveness and readily invite trouble by getting into brawls. If this is the case, it is high time that you get professional help before it is too late.

THE MECHANICS OF IRRITABLE MOOD – FIND YOURS IF IT IS

It is first important for us to understand the mechanics of anger before we understands about irritable mood and defusing it. There can be many stimulants for our anger and are different for each individual and depend upon situations and circumstances. However, the mechanics that operate are common to all and we will discuss about them.

1. **Your Visions May Be Clashing With Reality**: Anger most often is the resultant of our preconceived notions and expectations that we have from people and the world around us. When these do not find acceptance in reality, they upset our frame of mind and we feel disturbed. This disturbance causes us to get frustrated, leading to our aggressive outbursts. In short, we feel angry when reality does not match up with our hopes and expectations.
2. **Your Thoughts May Be Distorted**: Another related trigger of our anger can be our judgments of the intentions of other people. We may falsely believe them to be malicious or intentionally aimed at causing us harm or pain. This threatens us and we react in an aggressive manner. This type of warped thinking generally occurs when people behave in a manner, which is against our personal set of rules. Evaluating their behaviour, we arbitrarily decide that we clearly understand their hidden intentions, which obviously we perceive as malicious.
3. **You May Be Searching Reasons**: Many a times right from the morning one begins to find fault in the various things which are either there or not present as expected. Getting out of bed, you find that your slippers are missing and you urgently need to go to the toilets. In the toilets, the tap has run dry and the towel, which had been sent to the laundry, not replaced. Such things may surely be annoying but the slipper can always be located, water can be made available from the bucket or another source and a towel can be asked for. However, when we do not look for alternatives and tend to show our annoyance it is the beginning of looking at every thing with a jaundiced eye at least for the day. In short, we are giving ourselves reasons to be annoyed and then further annoyed.
4. **Your Perfection May Be Irritating You**: Many of us make our own life difficult and readily invite annoyance by trying to be as perfect in our works and expecting the same from others.

Perfection is difficult to achieve as every individual has his or her own standards of evaluating things. What may appear perfect to one may look distorted to the other. However when the expectations of people with a perfect eye for things is not met they tend to show their annoyance overtly or covertly. People who always want everything to be perfect mostly are unsatisfied and remain in an annoyed state.

5. **You May Have Set Too High standards**: Many a times we overestimate our own potentials and set up high standards for achieving. We have to really push ourselves hard to achieve our set goals and overcome many obstructions coming in our way. If we are incapable to overcome these obstructions, we get frustrated and thereby annoyed and angry. The secret behind setting up high standards is mostly not our own achievement drive but the meeting of expectations of other significant people in our lives. This attitude develops over the years and has a lot to do with parental and peer pressures to achieve goals set by them.

IRRITABLE MOOD – AN INDICATION OF DISORDERS

Irritable mood can be an indication of many psychological disorders since it is an important symptom associated with them. (*Most of these disorders have been dealt in detail in this book in separate chapters*).

1. **Neurasthenia (Mental Fatigue)**: Increasing mental tension or workload many a times produces mental fatigue. This type of fatigue is medically termed as neurasthenia. One of the major symptoms of this disorder is irritability. If irritability is coupled with other symptoms like feeling of fatigue, experiencing low energy levels, pain in the muscles, headaches, difficulty in sleeping and giddiness then they are indications that the person is suffering from neurasthenia.
2. **Depression**: The person is said to be suffering from depression when irritability is accompanied with changes in appetite and sleeping patterns; feeling of worthlessness, hopelessness, and inappropriate guilt; loss of interest or

pleasure in formerly important activities; fatigue; inability to concentrate; overwhelming sadness; disturbed thinking; physical symptoms such as headaches or stomachaches; and suicidal thoughts or behaviours.

3. **Anxiety**: When irritability is accompanied with an increased heartbeat, restlessness, coldness in hands and feet, difficulty sleeping, disturbing negative thoughts, difficulty in concentrating etc. then there is a probability he may be suffering from an anxiety disorder.
4. **Mania**: People suffering from this disorder begin thinking that they are better than others in all respect. They begin loosing control over their mental prowess and exhibit heightened irritability, which is dangerous and disastrous at times.
5. **Psychosis**: This is a serious mental disorder in which the individual begins to doubt people without adequate reasons. He feels that people are plotting and planning against him. It is because of this typical thought that he also becomes susceptible to irritability.
6. **Personality Disorders**: Many an individuals suffer from some personality disorder or the other ranging from mild to extreme. Such people exhibit arrogance, antisocial behaviour, emotional instability etc. Such people may also show signs of irritability.
7. **Other Conditions**: Other conditions where irritable mood can be associated are alcoholism, drastic and unexpected change in life, failure to achieve, inadequate sleep, attention deficiency and low intelligence, etc.

TAMING THE DEVIL OF IRRITABILITY

In most of the cases, heightened irritability is an indication of some underlying psychological disorder. If the problem is identified and treated then irritability is also cured alongside. For treating irritability associated with intense psychological problems, it is best to seek medical help. However, if irritability is not heightened then there is no need for seeking medical assistance. You can follow the simple advice and defuse your irritability. It is essential that you be determined to cure yourself and bring the required essential changes within you. You will not only have to battle with the seemingly hostile world around you but also with yourself in trying to stop getting irritated over things.

1. **Find The Triggers of Your Irritation**: The first thing you need to do is identify all the triggers of your irritation and list them out. These triggers are signals, which stimulate you and onset your irritated behaviour. Looking at a badly ironed shirt in your closet can trigger your irritation or any disturbance while doing work may irritate you. If you look around you will find many. This listing will make you consciously aware of what all instigates your irritation and you can be careful before you make a response towards them.
2. **Change Strategies**: Any thing, which brings annoyance to you, can be avoided by change of strategy. Suppose the road going to your office is much crowed and there are frequent traffic jams. Driving under such conditions brings annoyance to you, which, is carried forward, into your other daily tasks. You can best do is leave early for work much before the office rush begins, keep a driver if you can afford one or take a different route even if it is a bit longer. Changing strategies can help you avoid annoying things and conditions.
3. **Increase Reaction Time**: Generally, people who show heightened irritability have a very short reaction time. They react spontaneously without giving much thought. The best way to avoid getting annoyed and thereby irritated is take time to react to those situations, which are causing you annoyance. Your spouse is disturbing you by humming while you require concentrating on your work. Do not get irritated and react immediately. Take a deep breath and slowly let it out. Appreciate the tune your spouse is humming and politely request that it be hummed later when you can have all ears for it. Your work will be done and your spouse will also be pleased. A few seconds reaction delay can change the whole scenario.

4. **Change Your Attitude**: You cannot control what happens to you, but you can control your attitude toward what happens to you, and in that, you will be mastering change rather than allowing it to master you. Whenever you are in conflict with someone, one factor can make the difference between damaging your relationship and deepening it. That factor is attitude. Attitude is the way you mentally look at the world around you. It is how you view your environment and your future. It is the focus you develop toward life itself. You may be having a negative attitude towards the way people drive on the road and create uncalled traffic jams by manner of overlooking road rules but the fact is that you also do the same many a times. You also do many things which others do not like and cause irritation to them. There is little difference in people, but that little difference makes a big difference. The little difference is going to be your attitude at looking at things and the big difference is whether it is positive or negative. So change your attitude and adopt a positive one.
5. **Share Your Problems**: Many times the reasons for our irritability are our pent up emotions. We need to share our thoughts and feelings which when done provide relief to us. Sharing problems with family and friends will not only unburden us but we may also get assistance in sorting them out.
6. **Remember You Are Not Omnipotent**: Remember you cannot go and change the world and make people behave according to your wish. You cannot always have the last word in an argument. Every individual is unique and has the right over his or her behaviour, views. Give them their space, and you will end up breathing more freely.
7. **Remember Your Irritation Is A Weapon Trained At You**: Getting irritated will cause more harm to you than it will cause to others. It will affect your peace of mind and can create havoc in your interpersonal relationships. It can damage both your mental as well as physical health. So disarm this weapon and put it away.

8. **Express Your Irritation Gracefully**: Sometimes it is very important to express your intense feelings even if they are associated with your rage. Bottled up feelings can make us unhealthy and inappropriately expressed ones can create problems. Take the graceful path and express your irritability in a subtle manner. You have had your say and at the same time not offended the other person.

In the end, remember if you will call your troubles experiences, and remember that every experience develops some latent force within you, you will grow vigorous and happy, and however adverse your circumstances may seem to be.

Chapter 13

The Devil of Forgetfulness – Recall It

"You can't talk about remembering without mentioning its counterpart. It seems that as much as we do remember, we forget even more. Forgetting is not very bad, and is in actuality, a natural phenomenon. Imagine if you remembered every minute detail of every minute or every hour, of every day during your entire life, no matter how good, bad, or insignificant. Now imagine trying to sift through it all for the important stuff like where you left your keys".

"In the practical use of our intellect, forgetting is as important as remembering."

Forgetting is a problem, which every individual experiences sometimes, or the other during the course of his life. Increasing age also increases forgetfulness. We forget general things like where we had kept the previous electricity bills or passing down a telephonic message to the person, it was meant for. In the past to help us remember, we used to make notes of things in a diary and at times forget where we had kept that diary. Today with the advent of technology, we are relying less on our memory and more on the gadgets, which remind us of things to do. The mobile, computer, and the television can all be set to give reminders. All this technology though is very convenient for us but it is weakening our memory and making us dependent on machines.

At moments, we tend to forget but then suddenly recall. This means that the information in reality not lost but unavailable to us at a given moment. This means that forgetting is not actually loosing or erasing of information. It is a failure to retrieve information from our memory due to specific reasons. Thus to have an understanding of forgetting you need to first know in brief about memory, its processes and types.

MEMORY AND FORGETTING

The basic information processing mechanism of a digital computer is based on the working of the human memory. It takes in information, processes it in steps and stages, and then produces an output. In the same manner we take in information through our sense organs, our brain processes it and then, as and when required, we produce the required output in terms of behaviour. To put this technically, memory involves three major processes – *encoding*, *storage,* and *retrieval.* In order to form new memories, information must be changed into a usable form, which occurs through the process known as encoding. Once information has been successfully encoded, it must be stored in memory for later use. Much of this stored memory lies outside of our awareness most of the time, except when we actually need to use it. The retrieval process allows us to bring stored memories into conscious awareness. Forgetting can be the resultant of a malfunctioning at any one of the three stages. During the encoding stage, the *constructive processes* operate and the to-be remembered information is modified. During storage, *reconstructive processes* modify the already stored information and during retrieval, there can be a *retrieval failure*. Apart from these, various other factors are also responsible for forgetting including biological ones.

TYPES OF MEMORIES

Sensory Memory: Sensory memory is of two types – visual (*iconic memory*) and auditory (*echoic memory*), depending on the sense organ in use for the reception of information. At any given moment, we are bombarded with a host of information, which is made available to us through our senses. We do not however take in all the information but only that which captures our attention. This information is briefly stored for approximately 30 seconds (for visual) – 4 seconds (for auditory) in the sensory channels and then only that information which we had attended to and recognized is passed down into the next stage – the short-term memory.

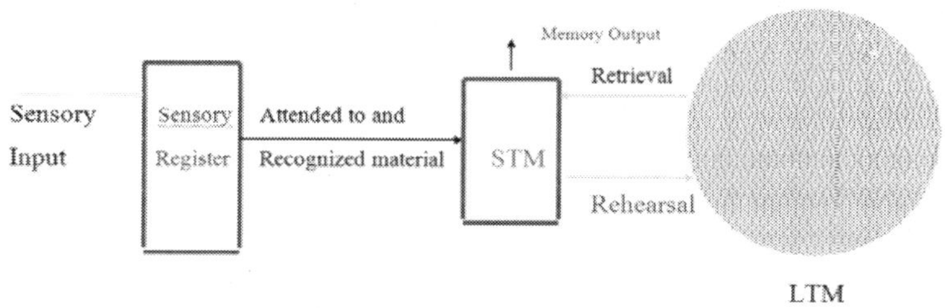

Short-Term Memory: This is the memory that holds information received from the sensory register for about 30 seconds, although the length of retention depends on a number of factors. The short-term memory has a limited capacity for processing information. This is the information about the happenings in the present thus; it is also referred to as the conscious mind. Most of the information stored in this short-term store is quickly forgotten and only that which we rehearse moves forward into the long-term memory. You must have had the experience of forgetting names and telephone numbers you just heard. This is so because thought you paid attention to what was being told but you did not rehearse the same. The way we rehearse is also of prime importance in relation to organization and thereafter its retrieval.

WHY WE REMEMBER WHAT WE REMEMBER

There are typically six reasons why information is stored in our short-term memory.

Primacy effect - information that occurs first is typically remembered better than information occurring later. When given a list of words or numbers, the first word or number is usually remembered due to rehearsing this more than other information.

Recency effect - often the last bit of information is remembered better because not as much time has past; time which results in forgetting.

Distinctiveness - if something stands out from information around it, it is often remembered better. Any distinctive information is easier to remember than that which is similar, usual, or mundane.

Frequency effect - rehearsal, as stated in the first example, results in better memory. Remember trying to memorize a formula for your math class. The more you went over it, the better you knew it.

Associations - when we associate or attach information to other information, it becomes easier to remember. Many of us use this strategy in our professions and everyday life in the form of acronyms.

Reconstruction - sometimes we actually fill in the blanks in our memory. In other words, when trying to get a complete picture in our minds, we will make up the missing parts, often without any realization that this is occurring.

Long-Term Memory: Our long-term memory is not an untidy jumble of unrelated information. We keep our memory store in order. We organize, categorize, and classify information in a number of ways. Our long-term memory is a bit like a library with a good cross-indexing system. Due to this organization, it becomes easy to search and retrieve information when required. You may have practically proved this fact many a times. Think of the times you have had difficulty recalling the name of someone you have not met or discussed about since a very long time. You tax your memory, searching for her name, looking for it in a specific category – example you have an idea that it starts with the alphabet "S" – you begin to recall it is Saroj… Sarojini …and then it strikes you it is Saroja. It had been at the tip of your tongue and you retrieved it from that specific category of "S". This *tip of the tongue phenomena* indicates that information in long-term memory is stored in organized categories. However, long-term memory is very stable but with the passage of time, we do tend to forget.

MEASURE YOUR FORGETFULNESS

This is a simple scale designed to measure your memory in relation to your forgetfulness. Read each statement carefully and then assign the "point" (0-3) in the blank space provided at the beginning of each statement. *The point you choose to assign is to be based on the frequency of occurrences with respect to the given statement.*

POINTS

0 – Never.
1 – Sometimes.
2 – Most of the time.
3 – Always.

____ 1. You forget where you kept your keys.

____ 2. You have difficulty recalling names of people you had met on previous occasions.

____ 3. You have difficulty locating where you parked your car/ motorcycle/scooter in the parking lot.

_____ 4. You forget your invitations/appointments.

_____ 5. You depend upon the reminders set by you on your mobile/computer/television for following schedules.

_____ 6. You request others to remind you of things to do.

_____ 7. You forget the birthdays/anniversaries of your family members.

_____ 8. You take the wrong road to places you have driven before to.

_____ 9. You forget the passwords of your e-mail account/net banking account.

_____ 10. After a brief interruption, you forget what you were saying.

_____ 11. You ask people to repeat instructions/information.

_____ 12. You immediately get down to noting down instructions/ information.

_____ 13. When you go shopping for vegetables/groceries, you take a list with you.

_____ 14. You need a calculator even to do simple calculations.

_____ 15. You have difficulty recalling names of places.

_____ 16. You forget spellings you had checked up in the dictionary a day before.

_____ 17. You forget to make payment to the shopkeeper after taking the things.

_____ 18. You forget what all you did during your last vacation.

_____ 19. You forget meanings of words, which you learnt a few days back.

_____20. When you visit your friend, you leave behind your things like books/keys/purse/hanky at their place.

SCORING AND INTERPRETATION

After you have assigned the points total them up. Their total is your score on this measure. If you have scored in the range of 46 – 60 you are *highly forgetful*; 31 – 45 *quite forgetful*; 16 – 30 *mildly forgetful* and 0 – 15 you are *not forgetful*.

IF YOU ARE FORGETFUL FIND YOUR REASONS

Forgetting is the difference between what one has learned and what he has retained. The major reasons responsible for ones forgetting are *retrieval failure, interference, failure to store, decay through disuse* and *motivated forgetting* apart from others.

1. **There May Have Been A Retrieval Failure**: This is also known as *cue-dependent forgetting*. When any information is available to us we add a cue or reminder along with it and store it in the specific category it belongs to in our long-term memory. When we recall that information, the retrieval cue assists us in doing so. However, at times, we are unable to do so because we had added an improper cue at the time of encoding, either the cue goes missing, or the proper cue is not available to us at that particular moment. This does not literally mean that we have forgotten permanently as eventually we do recall the information. Forgetting due to this reason is a very common phenomenon and occurs with every individual.
2. **Some Interference May Have Been Caused**: Throughout the day we are bombarded with information and our senses keep receiving them and our mind processing them in steps and stages, storing them accordingly in their specific categories. The multiple information, which we keep receiving, interferes with each other at all steps and stages. Prior memories interfere with newer memories and newer memories interfere with older ones. This is technically termed as *proactive* and *retroactive interference*.
3. **There May Have Been Encoding Failures**: Many a times our forgetting is because we never actually stored the information into long-term memory. This so happens because we never paid attention to the information and thus it could not be moved into our long-term memory from which we recall. All of us have seen a five-rupee note but very few will be able to recall what all is written on it. On the other hand, most of us will be able to recall the details in a five-hundred rupee note. This is so because we have minutely inspected one because

of its value. Our attention and related transfer of information into our memory is dependent on various such factors – both internal and external.

4. **The Information Stored May Have Decayed Through Disuse**: It is assumed that when we learn a '*trace*' is made in the brain known as *memory trace*. This trace involves some part of physical change that was not present prior to learning. With the passage of time the normal metabolic processes of the brain causes a fading or decay of the memory, so that traces of material once learned gradually disintegrate and eventually disappear altogether resulting in forgetting. This though is a hypothetical concept with little or no evidence but is one of the explanations for forgetting.
5. **You May Be Self-Motivated To Forget**: This stresses on a person's motives in remembering and forgetting. One aspect of this type of forgetting is the *principle of repression*, whereby some memories become inaccessible to recall because of the way in which they relate to our personal problems. Most of us try putting away our problems, which have created stresses or produced anxieties. At times, for our good mental health, it becomes essential to forget and then forget what we forgot. Psychoanalytic studies of normal people suggest that repression is a very general phenomenon.

SOME SERIOUS CAUSES OF FORGETTING

If you have scored very high on the measure of forgetfulness then you need to be watchful because forgetting can be the resultant of some minor as well as major psychological disorders. These disorders include - Neurasthenia, depression, dementia, attention deficit disorder, mental deficiency, alcoholism, dissociate amnesia, and anxiety. (*Most of these disorders have been dealt in detail in this book in separate chapters*).

1. **Neurasthenia**: This disorder arises when an individual get overburdened with pressures which in turn lead to mental fatigue. For example, doing excessive and undue work for

the sake of earning money, fame, and recognition. Apart from other symptoms, the individual suffering from this disorder tends to forget things because of loss of his ability to concentrate.

2. **Depression**: With the onset of depression ones attentiveness and the ability to concentrate begins to be drastically effected. This in turn affects his memory thereby leading to forgetfulness. Generally, depression effects sensory memory because of lack of attentiveness and short-term memory because of lack of concentration, which leads to lack of rehearsal and proper organization of information, which is to be sent for storage to the long-term memory.
3. **Dementia**: This disorder is generally associated with the age factor and found among older people. It is common knowledge that with increasing age there is also an increase in forgetting. Dementia may be because of the shrinking of the brain (*Alzheimer disease*) or because of the narrowing of the blood vessels, which supply blood to the brain.
4. **Attention Deficit Disorder**: This disorder is mainly found in children and youth. People suffering from this disorder become hyperactive because of imbalance in dopamine and other chemicals present in the brain. Such children are very restless and cannot continue doing a single task because their attention keeps fluctuating or shifting very rapidly. Their forgetfulness is also related with this fast shifting of their attention, which hampers information processing in the early stages itself.
5. **Mental Deficiency**: If an individual's intelligence lies below than that of an average individual, he is said to be mentally deficient. The onset of mental deficiency is generally from birth. It soon begins to reflect in the manner children respond to various events and things. They are slow in understanding, learning and in activities, which other children of their age

do and perform with relative ease. Such children also have a week memory and thus unable to remember things.

6. **Alcoholism and Drug:** People who consume alcohol and take drugs (barbiturates) on a regular basis, or are habitual to taking sleeping pills (benzodiazepine), develop a tendency towards forgetfulness.
7. **Amnesia**: This is related with repression and occurs in a dramatic way. The amnesia victim forgets items of personal reference while retaining a rich store of memories and habits to conduct current activities. The beginning of the amnesia can often be traced to some severe emotional traumatic events like violent attack, rape, death of loved one etc. or to physical shock/injury like head injury, disease, physical trauma etc. which the individual suffered from. The amnesia helps provide an escape from such haunting memories. In reality, there is no actual memory loss but only an impairing of access to information, which the individual has unconsciously blocked by the mechanism of repression. The memory related with other things function normal. Amnesia has two forms. A*nterograde amnesia,* in which new events contained in the short-term memory are not transferred to the permanent long-term memory. In *retrograde amnesia,* the person is not able to recall some memory or memories of the past, beyond ordinary forgetfulness. Amnesia can also be a mixture of the two forms – unable to recall an event prior to an accident (*retrograde amnesia*) and not remember what all occurred in the next few days (A*nterograde amnesia*).
8. **Anxiety Disorder**: If anxiety becomes very high then it can cause forgetfulness. This is so because when an individual has a high level of anxiety he is unable to register the information he is exposed to which is an important aspect of memory function.
9. **Other Causes**: Forgetfulness is also related with problems such as thyroid, AIDS, schizophrenia, severe head injury, epilepsy, tumor in the brain, deficiency of the vitamin thiamin, multiple sclerosis, diabetes, sleeplessness, cognitive disorder,

side effects of some medicines, chronic fatigue syndrome, during pregnancy and adjusting to a totally new environment.

TAMING THE DEVIL OF FORGETFULNESS

Forgetfulness is not a disorder unless and until it is associated with or a resultant of some major psychological disorder. If it is so them it is important to seek medical advice for the treatment of the core disorder. However, if your forgetfulness is the resultant of your week memory here are some memory enhancement tips you can follow. Remember memory follows the principle of use and disuse. The more you exercise it the more it sharpens and the better is your recall. The following tips are based on facts, which were discussed about memory and its functioning.

1. **Be Attentive**: As you saw that for information to be sent into the short-term memory from the sensory register, it was important that it be attended to properly. Without giving proper attention you possibly cannot expect to memorize anything leave alone forgetting it. Therefore, the first step is to pay rapt attention.
2. **Encode Information Properly**: When you are exposed to information, you tend to organize it into categories. Your proper encoding of information is very important for recall. Suppose you come across a new word "improvident" you will immediately associate it with its opposite "provident" and store it in that category. If by mistake or other wise you mix it up with word "providence", you will associate it with the same and wrongly encode it. On recall, you will search for that word and retrieve "improvidence" instead of "improvident". Thus, it is very important that you encode the information in a correct manner.
3. **Learn Things The Way It Suits You**: We though are humans and function based on some common psychological principals yet there are individual differences in our style. Some of us encode information best by seeing or reading while others find it more convenient to hear it and encode it. You should adopt the strategy you feel comfortable with – listen to a

prerecorded audio tape or read a book or notes. However, the best encoding takes place through a combination of both types – audio and visual.

4. **Do Elaborative Rehearsal**: Encoding though is important in the initial stages but rehearsal of the encoded information important for long-term storage of the same. If you are introduced to someone at a party and he verbally tells you his mobile number. If you want to remember it you will have to consciously repeat the digits of the number quietly for a few times. The same applies to any information you are exposed to and want to put into your memory. It is important that when you do rehearsal you should do elaborative rehearsal giving it organization and meaning. This way you can be sure that it will be stored properly in your memory and available easily to you when required.
5. **Add A Cue**: When we are exposed to any new information, we unconsciously associate it with what it relates. The best way to enable correct recall is to consciously make an effort and add a retrieval cue to the information at the time of encoding. Suppose you are learning Malayalam and told, that water is called "*Vellam*" in that language. What you can do immediately is add the retrieval cue "Well" to it because well relates with water. When later on you are asked what water is called in Malayalam you will immediately think of the well and pull out the word "*Vellam*" from your memory store.
6. **Enable Networking In Your Memory Device**: Your memory already must be containing lots of information about things in the world. When you are exposed to fresh information immediately, relate and connect it with the information already stored in your memory. This will broaden your knowledge and ease your search engine job enabling it to conveniently retrieve information you have fed into the browser in your brain.
7. **Enable Sharing**: In a computer with the enabling of networking, you can share information as well. The same applies with you. Your knowledge increases when you

share. This is so because while sharing you are giving fresh rehearsals to the already stored input in your memory making it stronger.

8. **Control Information Inputs**: When we are exposed to information, the constructive processes begin to operate automatically on their own, modifying the information, which is to be remembered. We encode what we infer and if this inference of ours is faulty, it may lead us to omit important details. Thus, while encoding information we must try switching on to a manual mode and encode the information taking care not to omit important details.
9. **Use Imagery For Encoding**: An important aspect of long-term memory is the way in which incoming information is encoded. Whenever we hear about anything, we try to visualize it – form an image of the same. This visualization helps us in encoding that information. These images are not exact copies of the input but partial and altered representations of what is around us. Studies have shown that when we encode information by forming images they aid in recall.
10. **Set Your Priorities**: You simply cannot afford to take in all the information you are exposed to throughout the time. There is a capacity to what you can take it, process the same and store it. Even a computer cannot possible process and store beyond its capacity. So set your priorities and focus on what you really need to know and store in your memory. This will also not unnecessary put stress upon your resources and your memory will function to its full capacity.
11. **Note Down Things**: Though taking help of notes or other devices for remembering do no good to your memory but they surely assist you in reminding you and not forgetting. However, you still will have to remember to make the note and key in the information in your device.
12. **Do Regular Exercises**: A healthy mind stays in a healthy body. Regular exercises will strengthen the body and help in

the reduction of your stress, depression, and anxiety levels. All these associated disorders adversely affect memory.

13. **Relax**: Relaxation will give rest to your body as well as mind. Your fatigue – mental as well as physical will go and your will feel rejuvenated. There are various relaxation exercises you can do like yoga, meditation, or just simply chill.
14. **Sleep Well**: A good night sleep re-energizes your systems, makes you healthy and wise. So follow a definite sleep schedule and sleep as per the requirements of your body.
15. **Say No To Smoking**: Smoking heightens the risk of vascular disorders, which can cause strokes and constrict arteries that deliver oxygen to the brain. This less supply of oxygen to the brain will reduce its capacity to function efficiently. So avoid trying to blow away your memory in smoke.
16. **Take a Wholesome balanced Diet**: Include in your diet food, which contains vitamin B6, B12, and folic acid. Vitamin e, E and beta-carotene and omega-3 fatty acids. All these together provide the required resources to the body for effective functioning. This in turn will also benefit your brain and thereby memory functioning. So feed your forgetfulness a proper and balanced diet so that it may disappear.
17. **Have A Positive Outlook**: The manner in which we perceive things makes a lot of difference how we will encode the same. Out negative outlook influence upon the inferences we make end up in faulty encoding. Having a positive outlook will not only motivate us to accomplish a task but also to be it with the best of our ability. This will ultimately also influence the manner in which we will encode the information. Learning something just for the sake of it will lead us to distorted encoding due to negativity. We will not pay attention and do proper rehearsals. So always, keep a positive outlook towards the tasks you have to do or learn.

Memory and forgetting is all about, our perceptions and feelings, thoughts and thinking patterns, our learning and our emotions. In short, it is all about how we perceive things; interpret them by drawing inferences and have emotional reactions based on past experiences. If we have a positive outlook towards life and the many negative experiences, which we undergo the memories related with them will not make us escape from reality. We need to develop in a healthy manner and remain living a healthy life. To begin afresh let us forget those things which are behind and reach forth unto those which are before – look forward to a good mental health and cherish memories, recalling them to share your positive side.

Chapter 15

The Devil of Fearful Dreams – Sweeten It

"All our fears and thoughts come out from the subconscious mind in the form of dreams at night and the mind itself seems to enter the subconscious realm during sleep. Fearful dreams are called nightmares, such dreams are usually fearful and intense, frightening dreams, which may suddenly lead the dreamer to awaken, the person who has a nightmare is so shaken and scared that he may remain frightened even when fully roused from sleep. Since such dreams tend to be so vivid and concrete in the dream, the person who is awake may still feel scared and may not want to return to sleep immediately".

"Dreams are the royal road to the unconscious"

All of us have dreams and they at times can be entertaining but at times can make us feel uncomfortable and frightened. Dreams, which are pleasurable generally, relate to wishes, which are not fulfilled in reality such as winning of a lottery, doing an act of bravery and becoming famous. Many a times, repressed sexual desires also find themselves being executed in the dream. There are dreams relating to hostility and violence in which the individual is taking revenge and emerging victorious. The dreams, which relate to sexuality and hostility, are generally latent urges of the individual, which if executed in reality would not be accepted by a civilized society.

Apart from dreams that entertain us or fulfil our thwarted and repressed unacceptable desires, we also have dreams, which terrify us. We see many a times in our dreams that we are falling down from a great height, drowning in water, being attacked by a wild beast and unable to move, being caught in a very narrow and tight space, finding yourself naked in front of others, unable to breath, not having prepared for the scheduled examination or such horrifying images and incidences we cannot relate to or make sense of. It thus becomes important for us to say good night and sweet dreams to people we wish well off.

PSYCHOLOGY OF DREAMS

Dreams are a succession of images, thoughts, sounds, or emotions passing through the mind during sleep. The content and purpose of dreams are not fully understood, though they have been a topic of speculation and interest throughout recorded history. People say we cannot sleep because we dream but Sigmund Freud tried to prove that people sleep because they dream. As per his statement, dreams are not impediments in our sleep but its facilitator. He saw all dreams as attempted wish fulfillment of some latent desires, thoughts, and motivations of the individual. In this manner, dreams are disguised fulfillments of our repressed wishes. He divided the dreams into three classes. *Wish Dreams*, which he related with unfulfilled desires; *Anxiety Dreams*, which he related with anxious moments one has experienced, and *Punishment Dreams*, which he associated with feelings of remorse and guilt. Even today, every nonprofessional associates dreams and their interpretation with the works of Sigmund Freud. However, not all that he said holds ground.

J. Allan Hobson and Robert McClarley gave another recent explanation of dreams. They advocated that dreaming occurred in the rapid eye movement stage of sleeping when the circuits in the brain become active. This in turn activates those areas of the limbic system, which are involved in emotions, sensations, and memories, including the amygdala and hippocampus. When this activation takes place the brain synthesis, interrupts this internal activity, and attempts to find meaning in these signals. This finally results in dreaming. According to this explanation, dreams are a subjective interpretation of signal generated by the brain during sleep.

Though this theory as against that of Freud's claims that dreams are the result of internally generated signals it does not void the claim that they are meaningless. Hobson has commented that dreaming is "....our most creative conscious state, one in which the chaotic, spontaneous recombination of cognitive elements produces novel configurations of information: new ideas. While many or even most of these ideas may be nonsensical, if even a few of its fanciful products are truly useful, our dream time will not have been wasted."

There are other explanations of dreams as well. Some say that dreams are the result of our brain trying to interpret external stimuli during sleep while others suggest that dreams serve the purpose of a tune up utility, cleaning and refreshing our mental processes. Still others suggest dreams to be beneficial as they are therapeutic in nature, serving to loosely connect in a safe environment, different thoughts and ideas, which are guided by the emotions of the dreamer.

Whatever be the explanation for our dreams the only fact that remains unchallenged is that they play an important role in our mental health, are influenced by our past experiences and present set of circumstances, and relate to many hidden conditions of the mind. They provide an insight into our unconscious mind, the interpretation of which, through dreams, may still be an issue of controversy.

KNOW YOUR DREAM TYPE

Dreams have been classified into many categories and types. Similar categories have been assigned different types of names and a few types marginally overlap one another. However, what is important that a dream is dream and will remain one irrespective of its nomenclature.

THE SO CALLED GOOD DREAMS

1. **Precognitive Dreams**: This type of dream is a Para-psychological phenomena and difficult to explain because of lack of scientific evidence. It is somewhat like an extra sensory perception but in the form of a dream. Such dreams relate to prediction about future events especially those, which can cause harm to the individual. This type of dream generally occurs prior to a scheduled event and acts as a warning sign. There have been many instances when people have dreamt a night before they have to travel that their transport vehicle met with an accident. The next morning they cancelled their travel plans and breathe a sigh of relief when they hear about the accident that occurred on their travel route or of the transport vehicle they were supposed to travel in.
2. **Lucid Dreams**: Though this type of dreams may also be bad ones but the good part about them is that they can be manipulated and controlled by the dreamer in their latter stage. What actually happens is a person begins to dream and then lightly wakes up realizing the incidence was unreal. With this realization and once again in sleep he takes over the dream, directing it according to his whims and fancies. This type of takeover of dream content many a times serves the

purpose of fulfilling desires, which in reality would be simply not possible. Example of such dreams can be flying like a bird, jumping from one airplane on to the other and all such acts, which we can call stunts.

3. **Spiritual Dreams**: These types of dreams as the name suggests are supposedly good ones. Either they give the dreamer an opportunity to interact with the Almighty or those loved ones who have left for their heavenly abode. When the dead appear in the dreams, interacting with them is a very satisfying experience for the dreamer. If the Almighty appears in their dreams, it is said to be a great blessing.
4. **Recurring Dreams**: These are reruns of old dreams and with many episodes; the dreamer can vividly recall every minute detail he sees. Strangely, this type of dream is a common occurrence and psychologists have related it with unresolved issues with which the mind remains preoccupied all the time. Another explanation to this type of dream is related with an unconscious fear that the dreamer has been experiencing. Since this, types of dreams are generally not very pleasant since they are the product of unresolved issues and fear which the dreamer is being perturbed with.
5. **Past Life Dreams**: This is another dream associated with Para-psychological phenomena related with past life and rebirth. There is a belief that every living organism has a past life – not one but many until he attains salvation. Accordingly dreams that occur have also been related with past life incidences of the dreamer. Parapsychologists and other researchers who believe in the concept of past lives and rebirth have claimed that memories related for each past life are stored in an individual's subconscious. He can recall such memories when he is in an altered state of consciousness and they appear in the form of dreams.
6. **Day Dreams**: Dreams generally are associated with night sleep and daydreams used as a proverb synonym to building castles in the air. In reality daydream is not at all associated

with sleeping but a visualization of things with full awareness. When ever our brain thinks in an active manner it tends to form a visual image of the same. This visual image is like a dream we are seeing with our eyes open. How daydreams are to be rated depends upon the concrete nature of thought generating the images. It can be either building castles in the air or planning to achieve some concrete goals. Concrete visualization assists us in seeing the future of our inputs where as abstract visualization only gives us a temporary sense of jubilation. It is in many concrete daydreams that realities have begun and achieved even the impossible.

THE EVIDENT FEARFUL DREAMS

1. **Nightmares** (Sleep Paralysis): A nightmare is a vivid, unpleasant, and usually fearful dream, which throws your body out of its normal state of equilibrium. Such dreams are related with situations of danger, discomfort, death, and many other psychological and physical distresses. Nightmares occur mostly in the early hours of the morning. After seeing such a horrifying dream, the dreamer generally wakes up in a startled manner with a vivid memory of what he dreamt. He is then distressed, afraid and filled with anxiety and finds it difficult going back to sleep. The reasons for having nightmares are more psychological than physical. People having unhealthy interpersonal relationships, a poor self-image, history of abuse, stress, frustration, and a host of negative emotions are susceptible to having nightmares. Factors such as stress, anxiety, eating just before going to sleep are some other factors. It has also been researched that people who are sensitive, trusting, and open minded are more susceptible to having frequent nightmares. This can be so because of the fact that they face more hardships because of their inherently humble nature and are unable to express their resentments openly.
2. **Sleep Paralysis**: Technically sleep paralysis and nightmares may be the same thing but they do differ on one count – that

is the mode of undergoing the horrifying experience. In a nightmare after seeing a horrifying dream the dreamers wakes up and recalling the content of the dream begins to exhibit disturbed emotional symptoms. In sleep paralysis, the brain of the dreamer awakens but his body remains paralyzed. Though being fully conscious he cannot move a muscle. Lying in bed, he realizes the strange things happening to him. He feels as if he is being crushed by a heavy weight that has been put on his chest. This state may last for a few seconds to several minutes. When finally the dreamer comes out of it he experiences panic symptoms and the realization that the distorted perceptions of his were false. The paralysis state at times may be accompanied by terrifying vivid hallucinations and an acute sense of danger. It becomes frightening because of the vividness of the hallucinations. Upon fully awakening, there can also be a hallucination of addition fearful images being present in the room. If all this occurs together, one has a nightmarish experience while sleeping, partly awakening, and then being fully awake. It is a triple nightmare. Reasons for night paralysis include sleeping in a face upwards or supine position, irregular sleep schedules, sleeping disorders, increased stress, sudden environmental or lifestyle changes and a lucid dream that immediately precedes the episode. Other reasons are generally the same as those for nightmares.

3. **Night Terrors**: Night terrors though are sleep disorders, occurring in deep sleep during the first third of the night, but related with ones dreams. During night terrors, people wake up sweating heavily, their hearts pounding, and screaming in fear. They are unaware of their surroundings and unresponsive to attempts to comfort them. They may not calm down for 10 or 15 minutes, although they return to sleep quickly once the episode ends. Generally, they do not remember what scared them, but rarely a person will retain a vague image of something terrifying. A few children and adults who experience night terrors will sleepwalk during the

episode. The reasons for such night terrors can be anxiety and stress before a performance like an examination or contest or harbored feelings of fear or anguish. Whatever the reasons be persons soon outgrow them.

DO YOU HAVE FEARFUL DREAMS?

All of us dream but very few of us remember them. However, we do are aware of the types of dreams we have – good or bad. We are more concerned with fearful dreams since they can be due to an underlying cause and not good for our psychological wellbeing. This measure will help you know the intensity of your bad dreams and you can use the tips given to help you avoid them. Read each statement carefully and then assign the "point" (0-3) in the blank space provided at the beginning of each statement. *The point you choose to assign is to be based on the frequency of the dream related experiences you have undergone in the past one, two months or even later.* This measure will not be able to exactly pinpoint the type of fearful dream you are having but will let you know if you are having one.

POINTS

0 – Never.
1 – Sometimes.
2 – Most of the time.
3 – Always.

_____ 1. Your dreams are vivid and realistic and they cause you fear.

_____ 2. You feel frightened after seeing your dream.

_____ 3. You suddenly awake from your sleep with a feeling of intense fear.

_____ 4. You feel anxious after suddenly awakening from your sleep.

_____ 5. After suddenly awakening, you feel as if you have undergone some acute distress.

_____ 6. You immediately recall your dreams upon awakening.

_____ 7. You wake up screaming from your sleep.

_____ 8. You gain full alertness the moment you awake after seeing a horrifying dream.

_____ 9. After awakening from a dream you have difficulty going back to sleep.

_____ 10. You see dreams during the early hours of the morning.

_____ 11. You see the same dream many times.

_____ 12. Upon awakening after a dream, you see things and objects in your room.

_____ 13. Upon awakening from a dream, you find yourself sweating.

_____ 14. Upon awakening from a dream, your heartbeat seems to be increased.

_____ 15. In your dreams, you actually feel horrifying things that are happening.

_____ 16. Upon awakening from a dream, you are unable to move for some moments.

_____ **Total**

SCORING AND INTERPRETATION

After you have assigned the points to the statements total them up. This total is your score for this measure. If your score lies in the range of 37 – 48 you exhibit *extremely high symptoms* of having fearful dreams; in the range of 25 - 36 you exhibit *high symptoms* related with fearful dreams; in the range of 13 – 24 you exhibit *some symptoms* related with fearful dreams and if you have scored in the range of 0 – 12 you do not exhibit symptoms related with fearful dreams or exhibit some very rarely.

FEARFUL DREAMS AND RELATED DISORDERS

If you are having fearful dreams very frequently then they are possibly an indication to your suffering from some psychological problems. The problems, which are associated with fearful dreams, are *anxiety, depression, mental tension or fatigue, and stress*. All these problems have been discussed in separate chapters of this book.

TAMING THE DEVIL OF FEARFUL DREAMS

Here are some tips, which can help you avoid having fearful dreams. Follow them on a regular basis and they will surely give you sweet dreams.

1. **Adopt A Proper Sleeping Posture**: The posture one adopts during sleeping is responsible not only for your many physical ailments but also for the type of dreams, you may have. If you adopt a proper sleeping posture or make some adjustments, you can control the type of dreams you have. The important part is how you set yourself in bed to sleep. Since lucid dreaming occurs during the rapid eye movement stage of sleep (roughly 90 minutes after sleep onset), it is essential that you are comfortable all through the night. This comfort though is largely provided by your bedding but your posture also plays an important role. With lucid dreaming, you can have control of your dream and enjoy the same. Here are some sleep posture tips to help you get a good night's sleep.

   * **Back Sleepers -** If you are a back sleeper, experts suggest placing a pillow behind your head and tucking another pillow underneath your knees. This helps to relieve pressure on your lower back.
   * **Side Sleepers -** Besides being the healthiest sleep posture, side sleepers also tend to have more success with lucid dreaming. Place one or two pillows underneath your head and neck to help ensure proper spinal alignment. Then place an extra pillow in between your knees to open up your hips and prevent your knees from knocking.
   * **Stomach Sleepers -** If you are a stomach sleeper, you need to tuck a pillow underneath your hips to relieve strain off your lower back and neck. Keep in mind that you may find it difficult to lucid dream on your stomach, so try to sleep on your side or back if you can.

   By ensuring that you are as comfortable as possible from the moment your head hits the pillow, you are likely to have more success learning how to lucid dream. What's more, with the proper sleeping posture, you are going to wake up feeling better rested after a good night's sleep.

2. **Follow A Regular Sleeping Schedule**: Many a times fearful dreams are the resultant of inadequate sleep or wrong sleeping habits. Following a definite sleeping schedule on a regular basis will help you sleep better during the night and thereby give the body its required rest. This rest in turn will energize you and give you strength to deal with your daily stressors and cope with the anxieties. (*For more detail see, sleep disorders*).
3. **Avoid Taking Naps In The Noon Time**: This is also related with sleep problems in the night and indirectly becomes responsible for you seeing fearful dreams.
4. **Take Adequate Sleep**: One must fulfil the requirements for the required sleep his/her body demands. If the body is not given its due rest then the devils of horror will appear. So give the body its due rest and prevent the devils from appearing.
5. **Go Slow On Things**: In today's world, we all are in a hurry to achieve our targets not caring what effect it is having on our psychological wellbeing. Stress is a major cause for fearful dreams. So control your stress and have sweet dreams. (*For more details on stress, see chapter on stress*).
6. **Adapt To Your Environment**: The situations, circumstances, and lifestyles of many of us keep changing from time to time. We as humans have a tendency to follow a set pattern, which we had set for ourselves. When any change, not acceptable to us occurs in our immediate environment we tend to resist and not accept it. This causes maladjustment and brings stress and thereby our fearful dreams. To avoid this we must learn to adjust ourselves with the changes and adapt to the new situation and circumstances. If we can change something, we should but if not then we should learn to accept the fact.
7. **Have Control Over Your Negative Emotions**: The causes of fearful dreams are more psychological than physical. A bad relationship, poor self-image, a history of abuse, stress, frustration and many other such factors can change your overall attitude towards life, which may directly impede

your overall performance. Such tendencies are deep-rooted in the mind and nurtured by excessive negative *emotions* (frustration, uncontrolled anger, bitterness, excessive shame, guilt, arrogance, envy, jealousy, greed, fear, suspicious nature, inferiority complex, persistent agony or melancholy, mental instability, escapism or shilly-shallying tendencies, communication apprehension, poor will power, low grasping, absentmindedness, sloth, laziness, dawdling, dodging etc.) They prevent us from seeing and accepting the life situations naturally. Negative emotions are primarily responsible for gradual declination or downfall of our normal thinking process. *Behavioural negativities* like fear, shame, guilt, arrogance, envy, jealousy, greed, phobia, and many other like that are considered an expression of negative emotions. All this negative emotions then appear in disguised fearful forms in our dreams and torment us. Lessening these negative emotions will ultimately help us have a healthy mind and healthy thought with good dreams.

It is time that we wake up to the many bitter realities of life, which we try avoiding by either running away, or repressing them. We feel that we have run away from them or forgotten them but they do not forget us and torment us in our dreams. So wake up and lessen negative emotions. Boost your latent inner abilities and mould your inherent behaviour in accordance with the existing situations and circumstances. Get rid of your worries, tensions, and sufferings. This effort will help you in attaining a peaceful mind. So if you have to dream then do so about how you can make and rule over your own dreams.

Chapter 16

The Devil of Mania – Subdue It

"The fast ideas become too fast and there are far too many...overwhelming confusion replaces clarity...you stop keeping up with it--memory goes. Infectious humour ceases to amuse. Your friends become frightened...everything is now against the grain...you are irritable, angry, frightened, uncontrollable, and trapped".

"A manic is a creature of strange moods who is always at the top of the wheel of confidence or at the bottom of an intense depression".

Mania typically occurs as a symptom of *bipolar disorder* - a mood disorder characterized by both manic and depressive episodes. Individuals experiencing a manic episode often have feelings of self-importance, elation, talkativeness, sociability, and a desire to embark on goal-oriented activities, coupled with the less desirable characteristics of irritability, impatience, impulsiveness, hyperactivity, hyper-sexuality, and a decreased need for sleep. A mild form in mania that does not require hospitalization is termed *hypomania*. It is characterized by persistent or elevated expansive mood, hyperactivity, inflated self-esteem, etc., but of less intensity than mania. Mania that also features symptoms of depression ("agitated depression") is called mixed mania.

Although "severely elevated mood" sounds somewhat desirable and enjoyable, the experience of mania is often quite unpleasant and sometimes disturbing, if not frightening, for the person involved and those close to them, and may lead to impulsive behaviour that may later be regretted. It can also often be complicated by the sufferer's lack of judgment and insight regarding periods of exacerbation of characteristic states. Manic patients are frequently grandiose, obsessive, impulsive, irritable, belligerent, and frequently deny anything is wrong with them. Because mania frequently encourages high energy and decreased perception of need or ability to sleep, within a few days of a manic cycle, sleep-deprived psychosis may appear, further complicating the ability to think clearly. Racing thoughts and misperceptions lead to frustration and decreased ability to communicate with others.

There are different "stages" or "states" of mania. For example, a minor state may involve increased creativity, wit, gregariousness, and ambition. However, a more serious state of mania may involve lack of good judgment, lack of ability to focus, and even *psychosis*. The victim of mania may feel elated; however, he/she may also feel irritable, frustrated, and may experience derealization.

IS THERE A MANIC IN YOU?

Take this simple test and you will find out if there is a little devil hidden deep within you. You will also come to know if that little devil is in a severely elevated mood or a depressed one. The test is in two parts. Read each statement carefully and then assign the "point" (0 - 3) in the blank space provided at the beginning of each statement. *The point you choose to assign is to be based on the frequency with which you display the characteristic traits in the statement.*

PART I

Points

0 - Never.
1 - Sometimes.
2 - Mostly.
3 - Always.

_____ 1. You remain in a state of excitement.
_____ 2. You remain in an agitated state.
_____ 3. Many ideas keep coming to your mind.
_____ 4. You are very talkative.
_____ 5. You unnecessarily laugh a lot.
_____ 6. You indulge in useless conversation with people you do not even know.
_____ 7. You talk about achieving the impossible.
_____ 8. You feel that all other individuals are insignificant as compared with you.
_____ 9. You feel that only you have all the capabilities to achieve targets.

_____ 10. You make plans, which ordinary people cannot execute.

_____ 11. You show sudden interest in religious/social/political activities.

_____ 12. You like passing down orders to other people.

_____ 13. You get very angry when your orders are not met.

_____ 14. You feel fresh and active even if you do not sleep properly.

_____ 15. When you go to a market, you tend to purchase things, which are not required.

_____ 16. You are very stubborn.

_____ 17. You do not like other people correcting you.

_____ 18. You tend to argue with those who correct you.

_____ 19. You fight/argue over small things.

_____ 20. You cannot concentrate on one thing for long.

_____ 21. You wear very bright coloured clothes.

_____ 22. You admire yourself standing before the mirror.

_____ 23. You have a heightened desire to indulge in sexual activities.

_____ 24. You are suspicious of the motives of other people.

_____ **Total Score on Part 1**.

PART II

_____ 1. You have feelings of loneliness.

_____ 2. You feel very sad without any adequate reasons.

_____ 3. The world around you appears lifeless.

_____ 4. You feel everything is worthless.

_____ 5. You experience emptiness within you.

_____ 6. You have a feeling that only bad things are in store for you.

_____ 7. You have difficulty making decisions.

_____ 8. You do not feel like doing anything.

_____ 9. You avoid interacting with your friends.

_____ 10. You speak slowly in a monotonous voice.

_____ 11. You answer to questions in an abridged manner.

_____ 12. You are not curious to know about things.

____ 13. You intentionally avoid people known to you if they happen to be around.
____ 14. Your facial express remains lifeless.
____ 15. You walk in a stooping posture.
____ 16. You tend to hear voices blaming you of wrongs you have done.
____ 17. You feel guilty of having done many wrong things.
____ 18. You feel your sins are unpardonable.
____ 19. You feel you are suffering from an incurable disease.
____ 20. You feel your body is undergoing peculiar changes.
____ 21. You feel irritability.
____ 22. You have panic attacks.
____ 23. You have difficulty in sleeping.
____ 24. You feel fatigued without adequate cause.
____ **Total Score Part 2**

SCORING AND INTERPRETATION

After having assigned the points, total up the same for each part separately. *Part 1 is your score on the measure of mania. Part 2 is your score on depression* (which is here as a bipolar mood disorder).

Separate interpretation for Part 1 and Part 2 scores: If you have obtained a score in the range of 55 – 72 **in either or both of the parts separately** you are in a *extremely highly manic state / extremely highly depressive state*; in the range of 35 – 54 you are in a *highly manic state / highly depressive state*; 17 – 36 you are in a *moderately manic state / moderately depressively state*; and in the range of 0 – 18 you appear to be in a normal state on both the measures.

Remember this is only an indicator to help you find out if you are manic-depressive. If you have scored extremely high or high, it is time that you take treatment and talk with your psychiatrist/clinical psychologist.

THE MANIC REACTIONS – FIND YOURS IF YOU HAVE ONE

Manic reactions are characterized by varying degrees of elation and psychomotor over activity. In fact, the manic attack is often considered a defense against depression. Three degrees are commonly delineated, denoting the progression of behaviour from mild to extreme degrees of manic excitement. Though these attacks differ in degree rather than kind, they merit separate consideration.

1. **Hypomania**: This is the mildest form of manic reaction and is characterized by moderate elation, flightiness, and over activity. There is a less need for sleep, and both goal-motivated behaviour and metabolism increase. This type of mania does little to impair function or decrease the quality of life. People with hypomania are generally perceived as being energetic, euphoric, visionary, overflowing with new ideas, and sometimes over-confident and very charismatic. Unlike full-blown mania, they are sufficiently capable of coherent thought and action to participate in everyday activities. A person in the state of hypomania might be immune to fear and doubt and have little social inhibition. People experiencing hypomania are the typical "life of the party". They may talk to strangers easily, offer solutions to problems, and find pleasure in small activities. However, the elevated mood and energy level typical of hypomania can be beneficial but mania in itself has many undesirable consequences including those of a suicidal tendency.
2. **Acute Mania**: The symptoms in acute mania are similar to those in hypomania but are more pronounced. This condition may develop out of a hypomanic reaction or may develop with little or no warning except for a short period of insomnia, irritability, and restlessness. The outstanding symptoms of acute manic reactions are irritability and elated mood, the increased flight of irrational ideas, the rapid and frequent alternation of thought, and the extreme psychomotor activity. Elation and pressure of activity becomes more pronounced, and the individual may laugh passionately and talk at the top of his voice. He also tends to become increasingly boastful, dictatorial, and overbearing, and may order everyone around as if he were a super-dictator. He also gets irritated very easily and indulges in violent and destructive acts. His sexual drive is

enhanced and he may indulge in obscenity. He also has a wild flight of ideas, which keep alternating and move to extremes – obscenity to religious to political to social. There may also be an occurrence of transient delusions and hallucinations.

3. **Delirious Mania**: This is the most severe type of manic reaction. In this, the individual is confused, wildly excited, and violent. This condition may develop out of hypomania or acute mania but more frequently it appears suddenly and with a few warning signs. The individual is incoherent and severely disoriented. He has no apperception of his surroundings and may have vivid auditory and visual hallucinations. It is impossible to converse with him or to hold his attention. He evades the most extreme psychomotor over activity, is violent and destructive, and spends his nights and days in restless pacing, singing, screaming, gesticulating and incoherent scouting. One moment he may refuse food and the next moment devour everything he can get hold of. His behaviour is obscene and shameless, and personal habits completely deteriorated. He is also extremely dangerous to those around him and may seriously injure himself. In short, he fulfills the popular notion of raving manic.
4. **Mania – Mixed States**: Mania can also be experienced at the same time as depression, in a mixed episode. *Dysphoric mania* is primarily manic and *agitated depression* is primarily depressive. During a mixed episode, the person may experience the impulsiveness, insomnia, irritability, and flight of ideas that can be present in a manic episode as well as suicidal thoughts, guilt, feelings of hopelessness, and changes in appetite that are common during depressive episodes. Mixed episodes can be incredibly distressing to the individual. It can lead to panic attacks, substance abuse, and suicide. In the mixed state there is also an increased probability of suicide as depressive individuals who are also manic have the energy needed to commit the act and the thoughts of depression that would lead them initially to suicide.

CAUSES OF MANIA

It is very difficult to ascertain the exact causes for mania. However, some of the causes have been identified, and they are being listed below.

1. **Heredity**: Mania can be transmitted genetically to the offspring's from parents. It has been found in some studies that the children of parents who exhibit manic symptoms also exhibit the same. Such studies, though very few in number, have strengthened the belief that there is a strong probability of genetic transmission of mania. However, it still lacks much scientific evidence since in many such cases there is also no transmission.
2. **Chemical Changes In The Brain**: Manic can also occur with the imbalance of some chemicals in some specific areas of the brain. One hypothetical cause of mania is that the amount of the neurotransmitter serotonin in the temporal lobe may be excessively high. Dopamine, norepinephrine, glutamate, and gamma-aminobutyric acid also appear to play important roles. However, this imbalance can be corrected with the help of medicines.
3. **Other Ailments**: Many times mania is the resultant of other physical and mental ailments like schizoaffective disorder, obsessive-compulsive disorder etc. Sometimes the medicines taken for treating depression can also bring an individual in a manic state. Medicines taken for the treatment of some other ailments can also temporarily cause mania, especially steroids.
4. **Environmental Factors**: Many a times change in climatic conditions also arouses or subdues individuals and they may become hyperactive or depressed. Changed situation and circumstances with which the individual cannot cope with, and adjust too, many a times, put people under pressure and stress, causing mental tensions, leading to aroused or subdued behaviours.

1. **Constitutional Makeup**: The physique is also an important aspect of ones psychological makeup. Studies have shown

that individuals who are thickset, well-rounded have a higher probability of being manic-depressive. In contrast, it has also been found that stocky individuals are slightly less susceptible to this disorder than are lean and slender ones.

TAMING THE DEVIL OF MANIA

Even if mania is not treated, it cures on its own in a few months but those few months are like hell for the other family members staying with the manic. A manic individual may exhibit some serious behavioural problems or indulge in anti-social activities, which may be of great concern hence he /she should be given treatment at the earliest. Hypomania cases do not require hospitalization. They can be treated at home. Acute and delirious mania may require hospitalization for sometime. If the disorder is bipolar then the depressive state requires much more medical attention and care. *The tips given here are for both the states.*

1. **Hospitalization**: It is desirable to hospitalize most manic-depressive patients. In addition to providing better physical care, hospitalization removes patients from the disturbing home influences and is a protective measure against suicide and irresponsible behaviour.
2. **Diminish Outside Stimulation**: An important factor in the treatment of manic cases is to diminish outside stimulation. This means that the individual's interaction with other individuals in the house or outside has to be drastically cut off. This surely is a difficult condition to fulfil, as you cannot just put away the individual in solitary confinement. The most effective way to achieve this without hospitalization is through prolonged sleep therapy. Sleep therapy, which though is less effective than convulsion therapy, consists of putting the patient to sleep by means of drugs prescribed by the medical practitioner for a period of a week, with occasional periods of wakefulness for feeding purposes.
3. **Shock Therapy (E.C.T.)**: This is technically known as convulsion therapy and much more effective than sleep therapy. It is generally given to cases of extreme depression. Convulsion therapy involves periodic induction of convulsions

by the medical practitioner. This is done by injecting a convulsant drug or by passage of an electric current through the intact cortex. Only qualified medical professionals can administer shock therapy, so do not try it at home or else it can be fatal.

4. **Reduction of Over Activity**: In the treatment of manic reactions, one of the immediate aims is to reduce the patient's over activity. This over activity can be reduced with the help of prescribed tranquilizers and antipsychotic drugs. However, with the reduction in the dose of the medicines there is a quick relapse of manic activities.
5. **Engage In Constructive Activities**: The best possible way to stop a manic from indulging in destructive activities is to focus his attention and direct his energies towards constructive tasks. He/she can be asked to record his memoirs, write an autobiography, or engage in such tasks, which are for the benefit of society.
6. **Time Is The Greatest Healer**: Time is the greatest healing agent. In the majority of cases, the disease runs its course and terminates in recovery within a few months in the absence of any form of treatment. However, it is still advised to seek professional medical help.

Mania though appears to be the most perfect prescription glasses with which you can see the world. Life appears in front of you like an oversized movie screen and you feel that you are in total control of its storyline – directing it as per your whims and fancies. However, once the movie is over you feel disappointed and dejected. It is thus essential to recognize the various mood states so that the individual can obtain effective treatment and avoid the harmful consequences of the disease, which include destruction of personal relationships, loss of employment, and suicide. It may take time to discover the best treatment regimen for an individual. It is very important for both the individual and his/her family, to work with a psychologist and/or a psychiatrist to develop the most appropriate treatment plan. Subdue your mania and elevate from your depression striking a balance in your moods.

Chapter 17

The Devils of Obsessed Thoughts and Compulsive Acts – Control Them

"The phenomena of obsessive-compulsive behaviours may be manifested psychically or behaviourally; they may be experienced as ideas or impulses; they may refer to events anticipated in the future or actions already completed; they may express desire and wishes or protective measures against such desires; they may be simple, uncomplicated acts and ideas or elaborative, ritualized patterns of thinking and behaviour..."

"Habit is habit, and not to be flung out of the window by any man, but coaxed downstairs a step at a time".

Technically speaking doubt is the out spring of a psychological problem known as *obsessive-compulsive disorder* (O.C.D.). Compulsions force an individual to think about something that he wishes not to think about. Whereas compulsions force an individual to carry out actions, much against his free will. In both the cases, the individual usually realizes that his behaviour is irrational but he cannot seem to control it.

Most of us have experienced thoughts of a somewhat obsessional nature, such as persistent thoughts about a coming trip, or date, or a haunting melody that we cannot seem to get out of our mind. In the case of obsessive reactions however, the thoughts are much more persistent, appear irrational to the individual, and interfere with his everyday behaviour.

DO YOU HAVE O.C.D.? – FIND OUT

This simple test will help you know if you are compelled to think about something which you do not want to think about and/or carry out some action against your will. This is not a diagnostic test but only a preliminary self-test to determine if you are experiencing symptoms of obsessive-compulsive disorder. Read each statement carefully and then assign the "point" (0 - 3) in the blank space provided at the beginning of each statement. *The point you choose to assign is to be based on the frequency with which you display the characteristic traits in the statement.*

POINTS

0 - Never.

1 - Sometimes.

2 - Mostly.

3 - Always.

____ 1. You think about certain words/images/things so much that you are unable to perform any other task. (O)

____ 2. You indulge in repetitive hand washing throughout the day. (C)

____ 3. You think about indulging in weird sexual acts with strangers. (O)

____ 4. You keep adjusting things to keep them back in the right position. (C)

____ 5. You keep thinking about tasks you have already accomplished. (O)

____ 6. You check the cleanliness of chairs/car-bus seats/ before sitting on them. (C)

____ 7. You cannot stop counting numbers while performing certain activities. (O)

____ 8. You repeat aloud what has been already spoken, although you try to prevent yourself from doing it. (C)

____ 9. You think about what your partner/spouse may be doing behind your back. (O)

____ 10. You wash your hands after opening/touching a door in a public place. (C)

____ 11. You count to a certain number before finishing an activity. (O)

____ 12. You inspect things, which you have used repeatedly. (C)

____ 13. You are bothered by thoughts of hurting or killing yourself. (O)

____ 14. You touch switches on electric devices and count them. (C)

____ 15. You ponder on one specific thing many times throughout the day. (O)

____ 16. You fold the newspaper properly if it has been left jumbled up. (C)

____ 17. You leave home, and constantly think whether everything is in order there. (O)

____ 18. You keep back things in their original place if they have been left elsewhere. (C)

____ 19. You think a lot about exactly how you will dress up. (O)

____ 20. You recheck the locks on doors several times in the night. (C)

____ 21. You engage in counting things without reason. (O)

____ 22. You get troubled if you cannot complete an unnecessary act. (C)

____ 23. You fear that you are going to shout some obscene word. (O)

____ 24. You rearrange things even if they have not been disturbed. (C)

____ 25. You think that some serious disease will infect you. (O)

____ 26. You check your e-mails many times a day. (C)

____ 27. You think of hurting or killing someone. (O)

____ 28. You adjust your slippers in a specific position before going to bed. (C)

____ **Total Score of Odd Items** (1, 3, 5, 7, 9, ……25, 27)

____ **Total Score of Even Items** (2, 4, 6, 8, 10 ….26, 28)

SCORING AND INTERPRETATION

After having assigned the points, add up the points assigned by you to the odd number items. This will be your score on obsession. To obtain your score on compulsion add the points assigned by you to the even number items.

If you have scored on either measure in the range of 32 – 42 your *thoughts are very highly obsessive / your acts are highly compulsive*; in the range of 22 – 31 your *thoughts are highly obsessive / your acts are highly compulsive*; in the range of 11 – 21 your *thoughts are moderately obsessive / your acts are moderately compulsive*; and in the range of 0 – 10 your *thoughts are not obsessive / your acts are not compulsive.*

Remember this is only an indicator to help you find out if you have an obsessive-compulsive disorder. If you have scored very high or high, it is time that you take treatment and talk with your psychiatrist/clinical psychologist.

COMMON OBSESSIVE THOUGHTS IN OCD INCLUDE

- Fear of being contaminated by germs or dirt or contaminating others
- Fear of causing harm to yourself or others
- Intrusive sexually explicit or violent thoughts and images
- Excessive focus on religious or moral ideas
- Fear of losing or not having things you might need
- Order and symmetry: the idea that everything must line up "just right."
- Superstitions; excessive attention to something considered lucky or unlucky

COMMON COMPULSIVE BEHAVIOURS IN OCD INCLUDE

- Excessive double-checking of things, such as locks, appliances, and switches.
- Repeatedly checking in on loved ones to make sure they are safe.
- Counting, tapping, repeating certain words, or doing other senseless things to reduce anxiety.
- Spending a lot of time washing or cleaning.
- Ordering, evening out, or arranging things "just so."
- Praying excessively or engaging in rituals triggered by religious fear.
- Accumulating "junk" such as old newspapers, magazines, and empty food containers, or other things you do not have a use for.

HOW YOUR THOUGHTS BECOME OBSESSIVE

Many of us experience *intrusive thoughts*, which are unwelcome involuntary thoughts, images, or unpleasant ideas and have the probability of becoming an obsession. Such thoughts are upsetting or distressing and they at times become difficult to eliminate from our consciousness. These intrusive thoughts, urges and images are of inappropriate things at inappropriate times. These thoughts may center on a wide variety of topics. Usually they are concerned with inappropriate aggression, or with inappropriate sexual activities and unanswerable questions pertaining to the existence of God and the meaning of truth. They can also be related with morbid doubts concerning the correctness of one's past actions and the true identity of one's parents, concerns over bodily functions to suicide or to the solution of some scientific function. When such thoughts become persistent they are a sign of obsession.

Such intrusive thoughts usually begin with occasional ruminations, which can at first be dismissed from the mind. Even at this stage, the individual may experience some anxiety at the immoral or anti-social nature of the thoughts and may make a determined effort to get rid of them. However, they continue to recur, and more desperately, he/she tries to rid himself from them the greater their persistence.

HOW YOUR BEHAVIOUR BECOMES COMPULSIVE

Most of us show compulsive behaviour, such as touching fence posts, stepping over cracks in sidewalks, scribbling while talking over the telephone, walking while talking over a mobile phone, or turning away when a black cat crosses in front of our path. These compulsive acts of us are not indications of obsession. However, when one begins to feel compelled to perform some act, which, even during the process seems absurd and strange to him, then it is an indication of a compulsive behaviour.

Compulsive behaviour is the outcome of irresistible impulses, which compel an individual to perform acts of a repetitive nature much against his wishes. Such acts can vary from hand washing, money counting, shoulder shrugging, dusting, and combing ones hair or even applying makeup.

THE INSEPARABLE TWINS

Obsessions and compulsions are often inseparable. Obsessive ideas frequently lead to compulsive acts, and compulsions are based on insistent mental ideas. An obsessive thought produces anxiety, which is then reduced by engaging in repetitive acts. Shaking ones leg while sitting is a very common thing and psychologically it is an indication of anxiety. The anxiety level within the person engaged in shaking his leg is high and he is reducing it by performing a repetitive act.

In some instances, however the twins may separate and obsessive thoughts not lead to compulsive acts. This condition is known as *purely obsessional obsessive-compulsive disorder*. It is an obsessive-compulsive disorder without overt compulsions. Individuals suffering from this subtype, rather than engaging in observable compulsions, might perform covert, mental rituals, or might feel driven to avoid situations in which particular thoughts seem likely to intrude. This strategy enables such people to fulfil both public and private roles.

HARMFUL EFFECTS - BEWARE

Obsessions and compulsions reactions are disturbing, harmful, and painful because the individual fully realizing their absurdity and senselessness is powerless to combat them or to inhibit them adequately. However hard he tries, he cannot free his mind of the ever-present obsessive thoughts or successfully resist performing the compulsive act. This in turn occupies his total attention leading to drastic reduction in work efficiency and the impairment of personal adjustments. The compulsive acts though provide temporary relief from anxiety but it resurfaces to quickly forcing the compulsive act to be repetitive in nature. This repetitiveness leaves no time or energy for the individual to attend to his other duties.

In some rare cases, the individual suffering from obsession-compulsion may be asocial and harmful. Irresistible impulses to steal or to set fires, known as *kleptomania* and *pyromania*, respectively, frequently lead to legal entanglements. In cases of this type, the individual actually does not profit from the acts. He steals because he has a compulsive urge to do so and sets fire to a place because of the impelling urge.

Whatever is the result, intentional or not, obsessive-compulsive disorder is considered maladaptive because it represents irrational and exaggerated behaviour in the face of stresses that are not unduly upsetting to most people, and because such patterns reduce the flexibility of behaviour and the capabilities of self-direction.

WHAT CAUSES OBSESSIVE-COMPULSIVE BEHAVIOUR?

Either the obsessive thoughts or the compulsive actions may predominate in a given case, but both are part of a total reaction pattern, and the causes are essentially the same and they range from psychological to biological to environmental.

1. **Substitutive Thoughts And Activities**: The obsessive-compulsive may defend himself from anxiety by persistently thinking of or doing something else each time threatening thoughts or impulses make their appearance. In many cases, the compulsive may of course be directed towards a constructive task, which is judged abnormal because it is used as an escape from problems, which the individual must cope if he is to achieve effective adjustment. In some cases, substitutive thoughts may be more complicated, and involve the *defense mechanism* of *reaction formation* – acting just the opposite of what they are thinking to escape out of a dangerous situation. Obsessive fantasies may also help satisfy repressed desires and provide a substitute for over action.
2. **Guilt And Fear of Punishment**: Obsessive-compulsive behaviour often seems to stem from feelings of guilt and self-condemnation. In some instances, the individual may attempt to counteract forbidden desires or be cleansed of guilt by means of compulsive rituals. Compulsive hand washing rituals often represent an attempt to cleanse oneself of guilt relating to sexual or other immoral acts. The classic example is Lady Macbeth's symbolic hand washing after her participation in the bloody murder of King Duncan. Her hand washing ritual aims at the cleansing of guilt for her immoral behaviour.
3. **Assurance of Order And Predictability**: A rigid ordering of behaviour can be temporarily adaptive in particular difficult stress situations. This rigid pattern of behaviour helps to prevent anything from going wrong, and hence provides some security and predictability. However, if the slightest detail gets out of order, the entire defensive structure is endangered and the individual feels threatened and anxious.

4. **Biological Cause**: Some evidence shows that obsessive-compulsive disorder may be a result of changes in your body's own natural chemistry or brain functions. Some evidence also shows that obsessive-compulsive disorder may have a genetic component, but specific genes have yet to be identified. It has also been found that an insufficient level of serotonin, one of your brain's chemical messengers, may contribute to obsessive-compulsive disorder. Studies done by comparing images of the brains of people who have obsessive-compulsive disorder with the brains of those who do not show differences in brain activity patterns. In addition, people with obsessive-compulsive disorder who take medications that enhance the action of serotonin often have fewer obsessive-compulsive disorder symptoms.
5. **Environmental**: Some researchers also believe that obsessive-compulsive disorder stems from behaviour-related habits that you learned over time.
6. **Genetic**: There is a high probability of this disorder being transmitted from parents to their offspring's.

PERSONALITY CHARACTERISTICS AND OBSESSIVE-COMPULSIVE DISORDER

Obsessive-compulsive behaviour takes place in the context of a personality characterized by feelings of inadequacy and insecurity, rigid conscience development, a tendency towards feelings of guilt, and high vulnerability to threat.

Individuals suffering from obsessive-compulsive disorder are introverted, sensitive, socially awakened, and intelligent. They compensate for their inability to make decisions and their feelings of insecurity by being extremely meticulous, punctilious, over conscientious, and orderly. They are precise individuals who make a habit of perfection. Time and money are carefully budgeted, meals are served precisely on time, bills are paid when due, and every piece of furniture has its special place. Everything in their lives is just so. Not content with regimenting their own lives, many impose their rigid rules upon members of their household and employees. Their puritanical standards and high ideals deprive them of the capacity to enjoy life and with people. Intolerant of human foibles and devoid of humour, they find it difficult to establish friendly relationships with other people.

TAMING THE DEVIL OF OBSESSIVE-COMPULSIVE BEHAVIOUR

Individuals suffering from an obsessive-compulsive disorder realize the need for getting the same treated when things get out of hand and beyond their control. This disorder can be cured with the help of medicines, which a psychiatrist can prescribe along with cognitive behaviour therapy given by a clinical psychologist.

1. **Behaviour Therapy and Medication**: The specific technique used in behaviour therapy / cognative behaviour therapy is called "*exposure and ritual prevention*". It is also known as "*exposure and response prevention*. Using this technique the clinical psychologist gradually teaches the individual how to control his anxiety associated with not performing the ritual behaviour. Suppose an individual touches things and immediately after washes his hands thinking that the object he touched was contaminated. Using exposure and response prevention the clinical psychologist might ask the individual to touch something only very mildly contaminated such as a tissue that has been touched by another tissue that has been touched by the end of a toothpick that has touched a book that came from a "contaminated" location, such as a school. That is the "*exposure*". The "*ritual prevention*" is not washing hands after touching that tissue. Another example might be leaving the house and checking the lock only once (exposure) without going back and checking again (ritual prevention). The person fairly quickly habituates to the anxiety-producing situation and discovers that their anxiety level has dropped considerably; they can then progress to touching something more "contaminated" or not checking the lock at all—again, without performing the ritual behaviour of washing or checking. Exposure ritual/response prevention (ERP) has been demonstrated to be the most effective treatment

for obsessive-compulsive disorders. Using ERP alone, one can become completely symptom free. However, the individual must be highly motivated and consistent. It has generally been accepted that psychotherapy, in combination with psychotropic medication, is more effective than either option alone. However, more recent studies have shown no difference in outcomes for those treated with the combination of medicine and CBT versus CBT alone. If you have obsessive-compulsive disorder, you can practise the cognitive-behavioural techniques you have learned from therapy on your own.

2. **Educate Yourself About The Disorder**: Educating yourself about the disorder is an important first step. It is also important to learn everything you can about obsessive-compulsive disorders. You can get detailed information from books on it; you can also ask your psychiatrist/psychologist to tell you about it. The more information you have on it the better will be your coping with it.
3. **Follow The Therapeutic Advice**: Follow the advice given by your therapist and practise the skills taught on a regular basis. This dedication on your part will effectively help in eliminating your obsessions and compulsive behaviours. Remember this is a challenge and it requires your commitment and daily practice.
4. **Be Socially Active**: Your obsessed thoughts and/or your compulsive acts can take up so much time of your time and make you a social isolate. This isolation will aggravate your disorder all the more. It thus becomes important to avoid such a situation from arising. You should reach out to family and friends, enjoy in their company, as well as take their morale support. This support will assist in your fight against the disorder and also help guard against setbacks and keep you motivated.
5. **Reduce Your Stress**: Stress can be reduced by practicing relaxation techniques such as yoga, meditation, deep breathing, and even aerobics. This reduction in stress will bring down

your anxiety levels. Alongside you will also benefit physically from these techniques.

6. **Laugh At Your Self**: Laughter surely has been the best medicine since ages past. You fully realize how absurd your thoughts and/or acts are. See their funny side and try laughing them away. Laughing at yourself will not only make you feel good but also subdue the unwanted impulses. So learn to associate laughter as a response to these funny but unreasonable impulses of yours.

So refuse to act on an obsessive thought and indulge in a compulsive behaviour this way they both will die of inaction. Do not cease to think and act. Cease to be controlled by your irrational thoughts and to do meaningless repetitive acts. Do not judge your efforts by the number of times you fail, but by the number of times, you succeed. The number of times you succeed is in direct proportion to the number of times you will fail and keep on trying. So do not give up and have a new obsession – not to give in to your irrational impulses and act upon them.

Chapter 18

The Devil of Imaginary Ailments – Ignore It

"Hypochondriasis is a mental disease and individuals having this disorder believe that they have serious diseases even though medical test show negative result. Normal body function or minor health problems are considered by patients of hypochondriasis as symptoms of serious disease. It generally begins in late childhood, ratio is same for both the sexes, and worry or fear lasts for at least six months. Hypochondriasis may result in depression, stress, impairment from social activity, problem in daily life or nervousness. Patients are not lying about their symptoms but they consider that they are sick. Even after medical examination they don't accept it".

"An imaginary ailment is worse than a disease".

Technically imaginary ailments are referred to as *hypochondriacal delusions*. These delusions are concerned with an excessive preoccupation with imaginary physical or mental diseases. Even in the presence of contradictory evidence, there are persistent complaints of ailments such as cancer, tuberculosis, or ailments related with the heart, perception, and memory. The imaginary ailment can be any disease the patient has heard about or someone known to him is suffering from the same. Hypochondriasis and the other somatoform disorders are among the most difficult and most complex psychiatric disorders.

Many times such individuals also state that their brain is wasting away, their stomach is gone, their blood is turning into water, or their bones are becoming fragile. The common symptoms in borderline cases that are associated with this imaginary ailments is the fear of going insane, loosing one's mind, or undergoing a change in personality.

DO YOU SUFFER FROM IMAGINARY AILMENTS?

This measure will help you know if you suffer from imaginary ailments. Read each statement carefully and then assign the "point" (0 - 3) in the blank space provided at the beginning of each statement. *The point you choose to assign is to be based on the frequency with which you have been displaying the characteristic traits in the statement for the last six months or more.*

POINTS

0 - Never.
1 - Sometimes.
2 - Mostly.
3 - Always.

_____ 1. You worry a lot about your health.
_____ 2. You think there is something seriously wrong with your body.
_____ 3. You check up websites for symptoms of various ailments.
_____ 4. You visit your doctor frequently for general health checks up.
_____ 5. You take precautionary medications for seasonal flues.
_____ 6. You complain to others about your ailments.
_____ 7. You are bothered with aches and pains in your body.
_____ 8. You are afraid of falling sick.
_____ 9. You complain that you have a lot of stress.
_____ 10. You change doctors because you are not satisfied with their diagnosis.
_____ 11. You have recurring fears about cancer/AIDS.
_____ 12. You feel people do not take your illness seriously.
_____ 13. You exhibit symptoms of some serious disease.
_____ 14. You suffer from various health ailments throughout the year.
_____ 15. You take health booster medicines.
_____ 16. You feel many changes are happening in your body.
_____ 17. You believe you know better than your doctor does about your ailment.
_____ 18. You remain on sick leave from your work/college/school.
_____ 19. You like it when people offer sympathy to you because of your ailments.
_____ 20. You are obsessed with thinking about your health.
_____ **Total Score**

SCORING AND INTERPRETATION

After having assigned the points to the items, total them up. This is your score on this measure. If you have obtained a score in the range of 46 – 60 you are *extremely high on imaginative ailments*; in the range of 31 – 45 you are *high on imaginative ailments*; in the range of 16 – 30 you are *moderate on imaginative ailments* and in the range of 0 – 15 you do not appear to be presently imaginative about your ailments.

Remember this is only an indicator to help you find out if you have hypochondriasis. If you have scored extremely high or high, it is time that you take treatment and talk with your psychiatrist/clinical psychologist. *Your high scores may also be affected by a depressed state so check your scores on depression. The same is with anxiety – higher the anxiety the higher your score on this measure will be.*

THE MAIN FEATURES OF HYPOCHONDRIASIS DISORDERS

- Because of misinterpreting bodily symptoms, the patient becomes preoccupied with ideas or fears of having a serious illness.
- Appropriate medical investigation and reassurance do not relieve these ideas.
- These ideas are not delusional (as in Delusional Disorder) and are not restricted to concern about appearance (as in Body Dysmorphic Disorder).
- They cause distress that is clinically important or impair work, social, or personal functioning.
- They have lasted 6 months or longer.
- These ideas are do better explained by Generalized Anxiety Disorder, Major Depressive Episode, Obsessive-Compulsive Discrder, Panic Disorder, Separation Anxiety, or a different Somatoform Disorder.

DANGERS OF HYPOCHONDRIASIS

It is easy for hypochondriasis to become a self-replicating cycle. Many of the physical symptoms of illness can also be caused by stress. Joint and muscle pain, sweating, nausea and skin conditions are a few of the more common physical symptoms that hypochondriasis suffers worry about. That worry can, in turn, cause these symptoms to worsen and new symptoms to develop. Hypochondriasis may also lead sufferers to avoid seeking medical treatment altogether, thus jeopardizing their health.

WHY IMAGINARY AILMENTS OCCUR?

Hypochondriasis is usually interpreted as an escape from life difficulties by a flight into disease. It is also a convenient method of *rationalizing* threatening defeat or lack of achievement. In some cases, an element of self-punishment is noticeable. The various causes are being underlined below and they range from biological to social to environmental as well as associated with other disorders.

1. **Family History**: Hypochondriasis may be the resultant of a family history of specific ailments. This may cause concern within an individual and he may begin to worry and exibit symptoms of the same ailment/s.
2. **Faulty Upbringing**: The way children are brought up plays an important role in their overall personality development. If parents are overprotective, focus much on even minor health problems, show low pain tolerance, and have impaired verbal communication with the child then they are sowing the seeds of hypochondriasis in their children. Faulty parenting styles give rise to feelings of inadequacy, insecurity, and anxiety within the child who then may resort to seeking attention and security through imaginary ailments. However, whether the seeds of faulty parenting styles may or may not germinate depends on many other psychosocial factors as well.
3. **Childhood Traumas**: If a child has suffered some serious ailment and has been traumatized by the same then as an adult he may begin to worry too much about illness.
4. **Life Stressors**: Life stressors, such as a major life change, can cause one to worry too much about his/her body or health. These major life changes can include moving, changing jobs or schools, divorce, or marriage. Death of a loved one can also cause you to worry too much about your health.
5. **Attention Seeking Behaviour**: Some people are very attention seeking by nature and use all methods and modes

to get the same. Many times these imaginary ailments are a result of seeking attention from others. It is also possible that such an attention seeking behaviour had been reinforced in the past and has become conditioned.

6. **Unexpressed Emotions**: People who have difficulty expressing their emotions verbally or physically may begin communicating using symptoms of distress. Children or adults who are under pressure to achieve and unable to express the same tend to use this mode of imaginative ailments for communicating their distress. Anxious or depressed people also sometimes begin to express their emotions through symptoms of such imaginary ailments.
7. **Media Hype**: Many a times the media makes a hype of an epidemic outbreak making the viewers anxious specially those who are more susceptible. The portrayal of the epidemic as obscure, incurable, and inevitable creates a fear psychosis and people begin to think they are exhibiting the related symptoms. The outbreak of swine flue made many people suspect that they had caught it. There were queues at health centers for check up. Many articles, programs, and advertisements related with cancer, AIDS and tuberculosis also become one of the causes of hypochondriasis for susceptible individuals.
8. **Untimely Death Due To Ailment In Family**: Many a time such events like untimely death of parents, siblings, wife or any other close relatives from a disease may make an other wise healthy and happy individual fall prey to hypochondriasis. These individuals begin to suspect that they are also suffering from the same disease, which caused the death of their loved one. Such a situation at times also can lead to panic attacks.
9. **Lower Tolerance For Physical Discomforts**: Many individuals misinterpret bodily symptoms by augmenting and amplifying their somatic sensations. They also appear to have lower-than-usual thresholds for, and tolerance of, physical discomfort. For such individuals a normal abdominal pressure is experienced as stomach pain. If they happen to sustain an injury such as a foot sprain then it is experienced

with significant anxiety and taken as confirmation of their worry about being ill. This is an innate tendency within the individual to exaggerate his assessment of vulnerability to disease and their appraisal of the risk of serious illness.

10. **Escape Mechanism**: Individuals facing seemingly insurmountable and insolvable problems take on a sick role to escape from the situation. This role allows them to avoid noxious obligations, postpone unwelcome challenges, and be relieved from duties and obligations.
11. **Chemical Imbalance In The Brain**: Normal chemicals in the brain help your brain do its job. However, the brain must have the right amounts of these chemicals. Having the wrong amount of normal chemicals in your brain may cause or worsen hypochondriasis.
12. **Because of Other Ailments**: Psychological ailments such as panic attacks and obsessive-compulsive disorders are possibly related since the core component of anxiety and its faulty mechanism of reduction are common in these disorders. People suffering from hypochondriasis may also be suffering from panic attacks and obsessive-compulsive disorders or vice-versa.

TAMING THE DEVIL OF HYPOCHONDRIASIS

1. **Learn About Hypochondriasis**: It can be helpful to learn about hypochondria. Understanding the condition can help give you a different perspective on your perceived symptoms. This can supplement the tendency in those with hypochondria to research specific diseases that they believe they may have. Only reading about diseases increases the anxiety and compulsiveness of the condition by creating more material to worry about so try understanding the same as well. Understanding will educate you more than just superficial knowledge gained through hearing and gossip.
2. **Have A Good Relationship With Your Doctor**: Having a supportive doctor with whom you have a good relationship with can be of beneficial because it allows you to rule out any

real physical condition and trust that the information received from the doctor is accurate.

3. **Try Shifting Your Focus**: The frequent behaviour of constantly monitoring health and symptoms can be a hard habit to break and may need to be countered with other activities such as exercise and other ways of promoting health. This shifts the focus from disease to health.
4. **Take Counselling And Undergo Psychotherapy**: Many sufferers of hypochondriasis are resistant to psychotherapy. This is because symptoms of health anxiety disorder include the genuine belief that they are ill or about to become ill and feel frustrated when others suggest that the problem may be all in the mind. You can take counselling, cognitive behavioural therapy and psychotherapy which will be effectively used for your hypochondriasis treatment. It will provide symptom relief while helping you deal with your underlying issues. You should also try discussing any other problems or issues, and not focus solely on the symptoms. Seeking psychological help can benefit you in changing your approach to the condition.
5. **Alternative Treatments – Make Your Choice**: Even though hypochondriasis may be difficult to prevent in a health-conscious society, in which people are constantly exposed to messages reminding them to of the various problems they may have. However, if you are determined to overcome your problem of imaginary ailments you can also opt to take complementary therapies such as *behavioural-stress management*, *acupuncture*, *hypnosis*, *relaxation therapy,* and *massage*. All these can help to relieve your stress and anxiety. *Cognative behavioural therapy* (CBT), *hypnotherapy*, *reality therapy* and *behavioural therapy* will also prove useful for you. They will effectively help you in reducing the symptoms of the disorder. If you have severe hypochondriasis, you can also take medication such as anti-depressants on the prescription of your psychiatrist. These also will help you in effectively alleviating your hypochondriasis. There is still more - you can opt for "*exposure and response prevention*" where you will be

required to make a list of their hypochondriacal behaviours, such as checking body sensations and seeking reassurance from physicians or friends. Based on this your clinical psychologist will develop behavioural assignments for you. You will be required to follow his/her instructions and accomplish those assignments. You will also be required not to frequently monitor your physical sensations or seek reassurance from friends, family, and your doctor. You will have to train yourself to experience the anxiety that accompanies suppression of these behaviours. The practice of yours to expose yourself to anxiety will have to be continued by you until you are able to manage the same. With this practice, you will find the gradual reduction of your hypochondriacal behaviours. Although cognitive therapy focuses more on thoughts and exposure therapy more on behaviours, both are effective in reducing dysfunctional thoughts as well as behaviours.

6. **Self-Help**: If you do not have a therapist, you can try to identify your feelings by yourself. Take this opportunity when you are feeling physically or mentally bad. Try getting into contact with your feelings. You may temporally become more anxious, but afterwards you will be more calm and peaceful. Follow these simple steps and they will surely benefit you in reducing your stress and anxieties – thereby your hypochondriasis.
   - Find an isolated room with no disturbances.
   - Lie down on a comfortable bed or couch.
   - Close your eyes and keep them closed.
   - You may be besieged with unpleasant feelings, which may become unbearable.
   - Do not let them take control of you.
   - Concentrate on your suppressed feelings bringing them to your conscious mind.
   - Do not be surprised if they relate to worries, loathing, shame, anger, fear, guilt etc.
   - They may look dangerous to you but they are so when kept suppressed.

- Now let the unpleasant feelings spread and make intensive contact with you.
- Use verbal and physical modes to express the unpleasant feelings.
- With the expression of these feelings, they will soon mellow down and disappear.
- Take out the pent up feelings on a regular basis using this format – you will feel better.

  This technique will help you to listen introspectively to what is within you and to search for what you feel and want. You will become increasingly sincere and true to yourself as well as give up on your wild imaginations.

Imagination is good if it leads to a concrete output but when it becomes illusionary, it turn out to be a cause for suffering. All suffer from some or the other realistic ailments but those who suffer also from imaginary ones make their sufferings threefold. Escapism through imaginary ailments is not a solution to a problem but a bigger problem for the solution. If you are prone to suffering from such imaginary ailments, it is high time you wake up and take control of the situation. If you feel it has got out of your control then immediately get in touch with your psychiatrist/clinical psychologist/counselor. They will help you in making your life a healthy one. Tame the devil of your imaginary ailments by not giving it its due.

Chapter 19

The Devil of Fictitious Ailments – Disobey It

"The somatoform disorders are a group of psychological disorders characterized by conversion of emotional distress into physical symptoms, or by symptoms of physical illness, in the absence of an underlying medical condition that can fully explain their presence. Patients with these disorders typically present to general medical settings rather than to mental health settings. These disorders can be represented by a wide spectrum of severity, ranging from mild self-limited symptoms, such as stomachache and headache, to chronic disabling symptoms, such as seizures and paralysis. The physical symptoms can occur in the context of comorbid medical and psychiatric disorders, requiring diagnostic and treatment interventions from both medical and mental health professionals".

"By believing passionately in something that does not yet exist, we create it".

Some individuals cannot express their heartfelt problems openly. Such individuals then begin to express the suppressed emotions unconsciously through various physical pains and ailments, which they begin to experience. They do not adopt this mode of expressing their suppressed feelings intentionally and are not at all conscious about the same. The frustrations, which the individual has suppressed for long, give birth to feelings of physical pains and other ailments, which have no organic basis. Such dysfunctional symptoms tend to range from sensory or motor disability; hypersensitivity to pain. When such an individual visits a doctor seeking treatment for that ailment, he gets an opportunity to express his feelings through symptoms of the physical pain or discomfort he is experiencing. Initially when the doctor or the family members extend their sympathy towards such individuals they unknowingly strengthen the foundations of an ailment, which in reality is no existential. Technically this disorder is referred to as *somatoform disorder*.

The somatoform disorders are not a single disorder but a group of disorders characterized by physical symptoms suggesting a medical disorder. An individual suffering from this disorder though exhibits symptoms of physical diseases but the condition, which generates them, is psychiatric. Moreover, these symptoms cannot be fully explained as a medical disorder or as an occurrence substance use. Such a condition creates quite a diagnostic chaos since it becomes extremely difficult for medical practitioners to distinguish between a physical and psychiatric source for the patient's complaints. Often, the medical symptoms patients experience may be from both medical and a psychiatric illnesses. Anxiety disorders and mood disorders commonly produce physical symptoms. These physical symptoms can dramatically improve with successful treatment of the anxiety or mood disorder.

TEST YOUR FICTITIOUS AILMENTS – HOW REAL ARE THEY?

The following measure will help you evaluate your physical ailments in relation to somatoform disorders. This is not a diagnostic test but only a rough indicator. The test is in two parts. Read each statement carefully and then assign the "point" (0 - 3) in the blank space provided at the beginning of each statement. *The point you choose to assign is to be based on the frequency with which you have been making complains of ailments in the statement* ***before you attained the age of 30 years***.

PART I

Points

0 - Never.
1 - Sometimes.
2 - Mostly.
3 - Always.

____ 1. You complain/complained of having pain in the stomach.
____ 2. You complain/complained of having a headache.
____ 3. You complain/complained of stiffness in your muscles.
____ 4. You complain/complained of having a vomiting sensation.
____ 5. You complain/complained of numbness in your hands/ feet.
____ 6. You complain/complained itchiness in different/specific regions of your body.
____ 7. You complain/complained of having a backache.
____ 8. You complain/complained of pain during urination.
____ 9. You complain/complained of shortness of breath.
____ 10. You complain/complained of heart palpitation.

____ 11. You complain/complained of experiencing pain in the chest.

____ 12. You complain/complained of not remembering specific incidences.

____ 13. You complain/complained of difficulty in swallowing.

____ 14. You complain/complained of weakness in the muscles.

____ 15. You complain/complained of experiencing dizziness.

____ 16. You complain/complained of swellings in different parts of your body.

_____ **Total Part I**

PART II

____ 1. You get anxious discussion specific aspects of your life.

____ 2. You visit different doctors seeking for a cure of your ailment/s.

____ 3. You do not have relief from your ailment/s despite treatment/s.

____ 4. You find it difficult to cope with your responsibilities.

____ 5. You find it difficult to cope with your social commitments.

____ 6. You remain in a depressive mood.

____ 7. You project your difficulties in an exaggerated manner.

____ 8. You feel apathy towards sex.

_____ **Total Part II**

SCORING AND INTERPRETATION

After you have assigned the points total them up separately for both the parts. Part I is your *somatic symptoms* (relating to the body) score and Part II your *psychological symptoms* (mind) score. First, let us interpret them separately. In **part I** if you have scored in the range of 37 – 48 you exhibit *extremely high somatic* symptoms of somatoform disorders; in the range of 25 - 36 *high somatic* symptoms of somatoform disorders; in the range of 13 - 24; *moderate somatic* symptoms of somatoform disorders and in the range of 0 – 12 you do not seem to be exhibiting *somatic* symptoms of somatoform disorders.

Now look at your scores obtained on **Part II**. If you have scored in the range of 19 – 24 you exhibit *extremely high psychological* symptoms of somatoform disorders; in the range of 13 - 18 you exhibit *high psychological* symptoms of somatoform disorders; in the range of 7 - 12 *moderate psychological* symptoms of somatoform disorders and in the range of 0 – 6 you do not seem to be exhibiting *psychological* symptoms of somatoform disorders.

Now total up Part I and II. This will be your total score on this measure. If you have scored, in the range of 55 – 72 you exhibit *extremely high* symptoms of somatoform disorders; 37 - 54 *high* symptoms; 19 - 36 *moderate* symptoms and in the range of 0 – 18 you do not seem to be exhibiting symptoms associated with somatoform disorders.

MAJOR TYPES OF FICTITIOUS AILMENTS – FIND YOURS

Four major somatoform disorders exist: conversion disorder (also known as hysteria), *hypochondriasis*, *somatization disorder*, and *somatoform pain disorder*. Somatization disorder is also known as *Briquet's Syndrome*.

Conversion Disorder (Hysteria): In this disorder, the individual experiences an impairment of his senses or ability to walk or move. This is so in the absence of any neurological basis and its onset is seen to be temporarily related with psychological factors such as stress or trauma. The explanation to such a disorder lies in the fact that the individual is converting a psychological conflict or problem into an inability to move specific parts of the body or to use the senses normally. There have been many such cases of individuals loosing their ability of speech in situations, which they feel afraid to speak. There have also been incidences of a loss in the ability to walk when they have to travel to a place they detest going. In such and other similar cases the exhibited symptoms contain the anxiety and serve to get the individual out of a situation he perceives as threatening. The resolution of the emotion that underlies the physical symptom is called the individuals '*primary gain*', and the change that results in the individual's social, occupational, or family situation is referred to as a '*secondary gain*'. The physical symptoms associated with this specific disorder may include a loss of balance or paralysis of one arm or leg; the inability to swallow or speak; the loss of touch or pain sensation; going blind or deaf; seeing double; or having hallucinations, seizures, or convulsions. Unlike somatization disorder, conversion disorder may begin at any age, and it does not appear to run in families. This disorder is most commonly found in small children and adolescents who are under parental pressure or under self-created stress to achieve good grades in school and college. Overprotective or over involved parents also act as sources for the onset of this disorder in their children. The child begins to constantly exhibit those symptoms, which had been reinforced positively in the past to become the center of attention in the family.

Body Dysmorphic Disorder: This is a relatively new category of somatoform disorder. It is characterized by a preoccupation with an imagined or exaggerated defect in appearance. The areas in which this defect is imagined largely are the face, or head. Other parts of the body associated with sexual attractiveness such as breasts in a female or genitals in a male are also imagined as defective. The onset of this type of disorder is usually during the teen age when the adolescent begins to get aware of his/her sexuality. In extreme cases, such individuals undergo plastic surgeries. A glaring example of this type of disorder is a famous pop singer who underwent numerous plastic surgeries and it is suspected that he died of an overdose of painkillers he was taking to fight the painful after effects of the surgeries.

Pain Disorder: This disorder as the name suggests is characterized by the presence of extreme pain in parts of the body. This pain can include pelvic pain, cramps, muscle aches, headaches, stomachaches, backaches, or even arthritis. In many such cases, the pain of the individual is because of some psychological factors but in many such cases, a medical condition may also persist along with the psychological one. Such type of a disorder is a very common one in the general population.

Hypochondriasis: This disorder is characterized by an excessive fear of suffering from some severe ailment or disease. This ailment or disease keeps persisting despite a negative diagnosis for the same. This disorder is related to the individual's stressful events and from which he is seeking an escape in the excuse of ailments or diseases. (*For details, refer chapter on Imaginary Ailments*).

CAUSES OF FICTITIOUS AILMENTS – FIND YOURS

There is no specific cause for somatoform disorders but symptoms begin or worsen after losses (for example, loss of job, death of close relative, or friend). A greater intensity of symptoms often occurs with stress. Somatic complaints can also be the presenting and/or comorbid symptoms of childhood depression and anxiety disorders. Conscious and unconscious worries can lead to somatic symptoms with a spectrum of degrees of severity in almost every organ system. Since the groups of the somatoform disorders are categorized based on symptom patterns, their causes as presently understood include several different factors.

Stress In Family: This is believed to be as one of the most common causes of somatoform disorders in children and adolescents. Disorders of the conversion type (hysteria) among young children may also be connected with sexual or physical abuse within the family.

Faulty Parental Models: As in the case of most of the causes of abnormal behaviour faulty parenting, styles or models play a major role in the cause of somatoform disorders. This disorder may result in part from the child's unconscious imitation or reflection of parents inappropriate behaviours related with projections of symptoms of an ailment, which as such is not there. The child, observing the parent closely, realizes that 'gains' can be obtained through the projection of symptoms associated with a false and fictitious ailment. He then begins to imitate such behaviour on occasions he wants to seek advantage or gains.

Poor Ability to Express Emotions (**Alexithymia**): One of the basic causes of somatoform disorders is the individual's lack of ability to express his emotions freely. Such individuals then begin to express the suppressed emotions unconsciously through various physical pains and ailments, which they begin to experience. They do not adopt this mode of expressing their suppressed feelings intentionally and are not at all conscious about the same. The frustrations, which the individual has suppressed for long, give birth to feelings of physical pains and other ailments, which have no organic basis.

Alcohol and Drug Abuse: Alcohol and drug abuse are common in patients with somatoform disorders. Patients may attempt to treat their somatic pain with alcohol or other drugs. Additionally, alcohol or drug intoxication or withdrawal may induce somatic symptoms of unclear etiology.

Genetic Factors: Genetic influences also appear to contribute to somatization. Individuals who suffer from somatoform disorder may also differ in how they perceive and process pain.

Psychiatric Comorbidity: It has been generally established that a person who has any psychiatric disorder is at an increased risk of having another. A few studies have indicated that panic attacks, major depression, obsessive-compulsive disorder, mania, and possibly schizophrenia are the comorbid psychiatric disorders most likely to co-occur with somatoform disorder. However, few systematic data are available to support this presumption.

TAMING THE DEVIL OF FICTITIOUS AILMENTS

Taming the devil of somatoform disorders is often difficult since they commonly do not accept their symptoms to be because of some psychological reason. They become angry and irritated when medical practitioners cannot find the cause' for their symptoms. Another difficult that is faced is the development of some real physical disease at the same time. Hence, it becomes really an uphill task taming this fictitious devil. Another difficulty that arises is that many individuals suffering fro somatoform disorders also have problems such as depression, anxiety, or substance abuse. These problems also have to be addressed alongside. The plus point in addressing these parallel disorders is that it leads to an improvisation in the individuals overall condition.

If somehow the individual can be convinced that psychological factors are contributing to, or are causing the physical symptoms then they can be given a 'talking treatment' such as *cognitive behaviour therapy*. Therapy will help such individuals understand the reasons behind symptoms, as it aims to change any 'false' beliefs that they may have, and it teaches them how to identify and deal with their emotional issues.

SOME GENERAL PRINCIPLES OF TAMING FICTITIOUS AILMENTS

Treatment of somatoform disorders depends on the specific somatoform the individual has. Some principles hold in the treatment of patients with medically unexplained symptoms. They include:

1. **Rule Out Concurrent Physical Disorder**: Since many patients with somatic symptoms are not immune to true medical illnesses, it is important that the fictitious ailment should be ruled out after consultation with a medical practitioner and should not be a cause of worry for the family.
2. **Treat Comorbid Psychiatric Disorders**: The prevalence of anxiety and depressive disorders is high among somatizing patients. Anxious patients are more self-conscious and tend to catastrophize bodily sensations, misinterpret vague and ambiguous symptoms of unclear origin to serious diseases. Depressed individuals have a negative and pessimistic outlook to their symptoms without the support of objective evidence. If depression and anxiety are present, then getting treatment for them will improve somatic symptoms.
3. **Listen With Understanding And Acceptance**: Although symptoms may not be fully explained by medical illnesses, listening to the individual's symptoms with patience and understanding, and accepting how the individual genuinely feels and suffers can be very therapeutic to the patient.
4. **Catharsis**: Allowing individuals to express their sadness, anger, and frustration can be very helpful. It may be the main reasons why some patients keep returning to the clinic despite their symptoms persist. Since the symptoms are in reality a deceptive mode of expressing their subdued feelings such individuals, appreciate even a limited time to share their feelings. Give the individual a patient hearing and let him express himself.
5. **Instillation of hope**: It is very important that individual's feel their physician will not give up on them and is trying to provide them the best treatment available. Chronic individuals

survive on the moral support from their doctors who through perseverance, continue to instill hope to their patients. So instill within the individual hope and faith in the medical practitioner they visit.

6. **Reassurance**: Reassurance is more complicated in these individuals. Premature reassurances like "All the tests so far have been negative. The individual can consider the statement "there is nothing wrong with you" as the physician's incompetence in understanding their problems. Family members can do reassurance in an empathetic manner like, "Having done all these tests, the physician is confident that there is nothing serious. We need to monitor the symptoms and with care and precaution all will be well very soon". Such a positive reassurance will boost the morale of the individual making him look forward in an optimistic manner.
7. **Treat the patient, not symptoms**: Some individuals have chronic patterns of complaining about their somatic symptoms. Dwelling on symptoms sometimes leads to a dead end. It is always helpful to inquire about their lives, social background, job, family situation, and recent life events and to show interest in the patient as a person. Remember that relationship is one of the strongest healing factors.

The imaginative ability of the mind can be creative as well as destructive - destructive to the extent of making a perfectly healthy mind dominated by fictitious ailments, which end up impairing any type of healthy functioning. Imaginations do become realities but such realities, which actually have no existence. There is no escape from what one has escaped and lands from a frying pan into the fire. Individuals suffering from fictitious ailments need to wake up to reality and stay in touch with it. It is only by facing life that one lives through it and not by evading it.

Chapter 19

The Devil of Personality Disorders – Correct It

"Personality disorders are pervasive chronic psychological disorders, which can greatly affect a person's life. Having a personality disorder can negatively affect one's work, one's family, and one's social life. Personality disorders exists on a continuum so they can be mild to more severe in terms of how pervasive and to what extent a person exhibits the features of a particular personality disorder. While most people can live pretty normal lives with mild personality disorders (or more simply, personality traits), during times of increased stress or external pressures (work, family, a new relationship, etc.), the symptoms of the personality disorder will gain strength and begin to seriously interfere with their emotional and psychological functioning".

One's greatest challenge is to control oneself.

How an individual talks; how he thinks; how he feels; how he behaves with others; what is his nature like; how he works; and what his character is like all together reflect upon his personality. All these traits though common in humans vary with the degree and intensity with which they are exhibited. It is this variation, which differentiates them from each other. Even though there may be some degree of similarity but no two personalities are identical. It is because of this variation we find that some people are suspicious, some are timid, some careless and some highly undisciplined. We also find some people who hesitate in expressing their emotion even to people near and dear to them. In contrast, there are people who are trusting, bold, careful, and disciplined and are full of confidence.

Whether ones personality is normal or not this depends upon certain patterns of inner processes and behaviour. When an individual, for an extended period, begins to think, perceive, feel, and behave in a manner, which is not common in the general population, he is said to be deviating from the normal behaviour norms. Such behaviours, with the passage of time, become rigid and appear in different situations. They are considered maladaptive because they create psychological distress and life coping problems for the individuals and society.

Every personality disorder is identified with a personality style, which characterizes the "extreme" parameter value within a normal human characteristic (Table 17.1). One can label an individual as having a personality disorder only when his characteristic or symptoms cause personal harm and suffering or create disturbances in society. However, if an individual possessing the distinctive personality style does not suffer personally and effects society in a negative manner then he cannot be considered as having a personality disorder.

TABLE 17.1

Personality Disorder	Personality Disorder
Obsessive-compulsive (*Note: Obsessive-compulsive PD is not the same as OCD*)	Conscientious, diligent
Narcissistic	Ambitious, self-confident
Histrionic	Expressive, emotional
Paranoid	Alert, suspicious
Borderline	Erratic, spontaneous
Dependent	Affectionate, loyal
Schizoid	Independent, secretive, chary, lonely
Anxious, avoidant	Self-critical, careful
Schizotypal	Full of foreboding, sensitive
Antisocial (diagnosis)	Adventuresome, likely to take risks

TEST YOUR PERSONALITY

This measure will help you know whether your personality is in a stable state or not. This is not a diagnostic tool but it will help give you insight into any potential disorders that may be having a negative impact on your life. Read each statement carefully and then assign the "point" (0 - 3) in the blank space provided at the beginning of each statement. *The point you choose to assign is to be based on the frequency with which you have been displaying the characteristic traits in the statement since the last six months or more.*

POINTS

0 – Never True.

1 – Sometimes True.

2 – Mostly True.

3 – Always True.

A (PPD)

_____ 1. When someone snubs you, you get emotionally charged.

_____ 2. You get emotionally charged when you fail to get desired results.

_____ 3. You feel people are criticizing you behind your back.

_____ 4. You accuse others for all the wrongs that happen in your life.

_____ 5. You doubt the integrity of your spouse/friends.

_____ 6. You feel that people are plotting and planning against you.

_____ 7. You impose your will upon others.

_____ **Total Score A**

B (SPD)

_____ 1. You are not happy with anything that happens in your life.

_____ 2. When provoked you find it difficult to express your anger.

_____ 3. You avoid going to social gatherings.

_____ 4. You like staying all by yourself.

_____ 5. You are not bothered about what is going on in the city/ world.

_____ 6. You do not show sexual interest in the opposite sex.

_____ 7. It does not affect you if people criticize or appreciate you.

_____ **Total Score B**

C (APD)

_____ 1. You do not care for the sentiments of other people.

_____ 2. You go against the social norms and do as you please.

_____ 3. You do not regret after causing harm to others.

____ 4. You fight over trivial matters.
____ 5. You do life-defying acts not bothering for self or others.
____ 6. You enjoy indulging in petty criminal acts.
____ 7. You are impulsive and irresponsible in you decision-making.
____ **Total Score C**

D (EUPD)

____ 1. You readily get into a fight/argument with others.
____ 2. You take decisions without considering the pros and cons.
____ 3. You get angry when you hear anything being said against you.
____ 4. You spend your money freely without giving a second thought.
____ 5. You feel lonely and dejected.
____ 6. You threaten to hurt your self physically if your demands are not met.
____ 7. You drive your vehicle very rashly.
____ **Total Score D**

E (HPD)

____ 1. You like being the center of attention wherever you go.
____ 2. You greet all people in such an emotional manner as if you are meeting them after ages.
____ 3. You act in behave in a manner to attract attention of others.
____ 4. You are engaged in tasks for the satisfaction of your ego.
____ 5. You readily agree to what others say.
____ 6. You tend to express your emotions in a loud manner.
____ 7. You boost about your doings amongst your friends/ acquaintances.
____ **Total Score E**

F (O-C PD)

____ 1. You take a lot of precaution while even doing minor things.

_____ 2. You follow a fixed schedule in your daily life.
_____ 3. You try bringing perfection in all that you do.
_____ 4. You adhere to your high moral values even if they are causing a loss to you.
_____ 5. You do not pass down your work to others due to lack of trust in them.
_____ 6. You strictly follow rules and regulations.
_____ 7. You have a rigid attitude towards life and things.
_____ **Total Score F**

G (AxPD)

_____ 1. You feel yourself as inferior to others.
_____ 2. You remain in a state of tension.
_____ 3. You avoid meeting people after being insulted or ignored by them.
_____ 4. You freely interact with only those people whom you feel are trustworthy.
_____ 5. You are unable to express yourself before others.
_____ 6. You lack confidence while interacting with people.
_____ 7. You get disturbed if someone cracks a joke on you.
_____ **Total Score G**

H (DPD)

_____ 1. You rely on others to take your decisions.
_____ 2. You depend upon others for accomplishment of your tasks.
_____ 3. You remain very timid.
_____ 4. You go out of your way to please those people on whom you are dependent.
_____ 5. You take advice from others for even minor issues.
_____ 6. You feel insecure when you are left on our own.
_____ 7. You feel insecure thinking that people on whom you depend upon may leave you.
_____ **Total Score H**

I (DpPD)

_____ 1. You have a pessimistic attitude towards life.
_____ 2. You keep finding fault with yourself/ situations/ circumstances.

____ 3. You find it hard to take a decision.
____ 4. You are unable to experience the happiness as other people do.
____ 5. You remain in a depressed mood.
____ 6. You lack self-confidence in what ever you do.
____ 7. You lack initiative to do something new in your life.
____ **Total Score I**

J (NPD)

____ 1. You feel you are a very important person.
____ 2. You cannot tolerate hearing anything even minor against you.
____ 3. You are highly motivated to achieve name and fame.
____ 4. You do not value comments and suggestions of others.
____ 5. You do not empathize with the problems of other people.
____ 6. You feel depressed at times.
____ 7. You are only concerned about your achievements.
____ **Total Score J**

SCORING

After having assigned the points to the statements, total up each section separately. The interpretation of scores is the same for all the given personality disorders. (The alphabet codes assigned to the disorders are being decoded and discussed with their interpretation after the scoring). If you have scored in the range of 16 – 21 you are *extremely high* on that specific personality disorder; 11 -15 *high*; 6 – 10 *moderate* and 0 – 5 you do not seem to have that personality disorder. Remember this is only an indicator to help you find out if you have a personality disorder. If you have scored extremely high or high, it is time that you take treatment and talk with your psychiatrist/clinical psychologist.

PERSONALITY DISORDERS: FIND YOUR INTERPRETATION

A. Paranoid Personality Disorder: Individuals with this type of personality disorder do not trust others. They constantly suspect that people around them have sinister motives. They also tend to have excessive trust in their own knowledge and abilities and usually avoid close relationships. They search for hidden meanings in everything and read hostile intentions into the actions of others. They are quick to challenge the loyalties of friends, loved ones, and often appear cold and distant. They usually shift blame to other people and tend to carry long grudges.

B. **Schizoid Personality Disorder**: People with schizoid personality disorder avoid relationships and do not show much emotion. Unlike avoidants, schizoids genuinely prefer to be alone and do not secretly wish for popularity. They tend to seek jobs that require little social contact. Their social skills are often weak and they do not show a need for attention or acceptance. They are perceived by others as humourless and distant and often are termed "loners."

C. **Antisocial Personality Disorder**: A common misconception is that antisocial personality disorder refers to people who have poor social skills. The opposite is often the case. Instead, antisocial personality disorder is characterized by a lack of conscience. Individuals with this disorder are prone to criminal behaviour, believing that their victims are weak and deserving of being taken advantage of. Antisocial individuals tend to lie and steal. Often, they are careless with money and take action without thinking about consequences. They are often aggressive and are much more concerned with their own needs than the needs of others.

D. **Emotionally Unstable (Borderline) Personality Disorder**: Borderline personality disorder is characterized by mood instability and poor self-image. Individuals with this disorder are prone to constant mood swings and bouts of anger. Often, they will take their anger out on themselves, causing injury to their own body. Suicidal threats and actions are not uncommon. Borderlines think in very black and white terms and often form intense, conflict-ridden relationships. They are quick to anger when their expectations are not met. There is also an intense fear of abandonment with this disorder that interferes with many aspects if the individual's life. This fear often acts as a self-fulfilling prophecy as they cling to others, are very needy, feel helpless, and become overly involved and immediately attached. When the fear of abandonment becomes overwhelming, they will often push others out of their life as if trying to avoid being rejected. The cycle most often continues as the individual will then try everything to get people back in his or her life and once again becomes clingy, needy, and helpless.

E. **Histrionic Personality Disorder**: Individuals with histrionic personality disorder often come across as attention seeking or overly dramatic. They may be inclined to express their emotions in an exaggerated or theatrical manner and they are often seen as self-centered or overly concerned about their physical appearance. While their behaviour is often charming and inviting at first (as their enthusiasm and seductiveness is appealing), their relationships often remain shallow and may be short-lived once people realize their constant demand for attention and lack of authenticity. For these reasons, individuals with this disorder often function well socially or at work, but may have difficulties in inter-personal relationships. Such individuals constantly seeking approval or reassurance, are overly dramatic behaviour with exaggerated expressions of emotion and excessive sensitivity to criticism or disapproval. They are inappropriately sexually provocative, and their appearance and behaviour seductive. Alongside this they also have a tendency to consider relationships more intimate than they are. They are overly concerned with physical appearance, often using it to gain attention and feel uncomfortable if they are not the center of attention reflecting upon their self-centeredness. They tend to get easily frustrated and expresses low tolerance for delayed gratification. Their emotional expression is shallow and rapidly shifting. Along with this they are also easily influenced by others and suggestible, have a tendency to make rash decisions grounded on emotional impulse and may threaten or attempt suicide to get attention. As with other personality disorders, people with histrionic personality disorder usually only seek treatment when high stress levels or other situational factors in their lives become overwhelming and they begin to struggle with interpersonal relationships or feel that they are unable to cope.

F. **Obsessive-Compulsive Personality Disorder**: This individual is a perfectionist, and obsesses about details to the point of following rules for the sake of the rules. They are extremely inflexible. Their quest for perfection usually slows progress toward goals because they tend to re-do things forever, without ever completing anything. They are over conscientious at work, but tend to not have many relationships. They are extremely rigid in terms of morals and values, to a degree not expected by their religious background. Their perfectionism prevents them from delegating tasks to others, so they tend to be bogged down in details, and become overwhelmed. At times, they are afraid to throw anything away, for fear, they may need it someday, and they are sometimes truepenny pinchers. They often have difficulty making decisions, because of fear of making a mistake. This disorder should not be confused with conscientious behaviour, attention to detail, and a desire to do a good job. It should also not be confused with normal conservative morals and values, and a desire to save money for the future. These are all positive characteristics that actually assist an individual in coping with the world. Obsessive-compulsive personality disorder is a condition in which these traits are severely exaggerated to the point of becoming negative.

G. **Anxious Personality Disorder**: Individuals with an anxious personality disorder are overly sensitive to rejection, and they fear starting relationships or anything new. They have a strong desire for affection and acceptance but avoid intimate relationships and social situations for fear of disappointment and criticism. Unlike those with a schizoid personality, they are openly distressed by their isolation and inability to relate comfortably to others. Unlike those with a borderline personality, they do not respond to rejection with anger; instead, they withdraw and appear shy and timid. Anxious personality is similar to generalized social phobia.

H. **Dependent Personality Disorder**: Dependent personality disorder is a chronic condition involving over-reliance on others to meet emotional and physical needs. This pervasive and excessive need to be taken care of leads to a submissive and clinging behaviour as well as fears of separation. Individuals with dependent personality disorder have great difficulty even making every day's minor decisions without an excessive amount of advice and reassurance from others. These individuals tend to be passive and allow other people to take the initiative and assume responsibility for most major areas of their lives. Because they fear losing support or approval, individuals with dependent personality disorder often have difficulty expressing disagreement with other people, especially those on whom they are dependent. These individuals feel so unable to function alone that they will agree with things that they feel are wrong rather than risk losing the help of those to whom they look for guidance. Individuals with this disorder have difficulty initiating projects or doing things independently. They may go to excessive lengths to obtain nurturance and support from others, even to the point of volunteering for unpleasant tasks if such behaviour will bring the care that they need. Individuals with this disorder feel uncomfortable or helpless when alone, because of their exaggerated fears of being unable to care for themselves. When a close relationship ends individuals with dependent personality disorder may urgently seek another relationship to provide the care and support they need. They are often preoccupied with fears of being left to care for themselves.

I. **Depressive Personality Disorder**: Individuals suffering from this disorder have pervasive and continuous depressive thoughts and behaviours. They manifest themselves in every area of life and never decrease. The individual is gloomy, dejected, pessimistic, overly serious, lacks a sense of humour, cheerless, joyless, and constantly unhappy. This dark mood is not influenced by changing circumstances. The individual's self-image is distorted: he holds himself to be worthless, inadequate, a loser. His sense of self-worth and his self-esteem are invariably and unrealistically low. This feeling borders on self-hatred and self-abnegation leading to punishing himself unnecessarily. He is insulting towards his self, blaming and self-critical and is busy in hateful self-destruction. The individual also extends this tendency to humiliate and punish his nearest and dearest. His masochism is complemented by equally exacting sadism. He is negativistic, passive-aggressive, critical, judgmental, and disciplinary towards others. Such recurrent outbursts are followed by feelings of remorse and guilt, often coupled with over-sentimental and straight apologies. Individuals with a depressive personality disorder are also prone to excessive worry and brooding.

J. **Narcissistic Personality Disorder**: An individual with this disorder is in love with himself/herself, and has little positive regard for others other than in a superficial manner. They tend to be flashy in their presentation of themselves, seek, and demand admiration from others. They believe they are special and deserve special treatment, regardless of the problems this creates for others. They readily take advantage of others, and tend to be quite arrogant. In actuality, they are very sensitive, and tend not to be able to tolerate any criticism or negative feedback. They usually seek treatment because they are frustrated in getting what they want. However, they often do not seek treatment, because they perceive everyone else as causing the problems, not themselves.

HOW DO PERSONALITY DISORDERS DEVELOP?

The causation of any particular personality disorder is tremendously complex, and even with the information we do have it is all but impossible to predict how given circumstances will affect given individuals. It is not always possible to isolate and evaluate the multiple factors involved. However, I shall attempt to delineate the role that several kinds of biological, psychological, and socio-cultural factors can play in causing maladaptive behaviours, either by producing faulty development – thus hampering our adjustive demands – or by increasing stress or both. These factors are overall responsible for not only personality disorders but also all types of abnormal behaviours. (*All causes of abnormal behaviour/personality disorders are dealt with in the chapter on Causes of Abnormal Behaviour*).

1. **Biological Factors**: Biological factors influence all aspects of our behaviour, including our intellectual capabilities, basic temperament, primary reaction tendencies, stress tolerance, and adaptive resources. Thus, a wide range of biological conditions such as faulty genes, diseases, endocrine imbalances, malnutrition, injuries, and other conditions that interfere with normal development and functioning are potential causes of abnormal behaviours. In this manner, for example, genetically transmitted traits related with temperament can influence upon the way the child manages stressful situations and other threatening impulses. These and many others inherited characteristics ultimately end up shaping his over all personality. If there is a genetic aberration then it will result in the development of faulty coping strategies, negatively influencing the personality.
2. **Faulty Upbringing**: The development of one's personality is dependent upon and influenced by heredity and the environment. Heredity is like clay, which provides the core components and environment the potter, which shapes the ultimate personality. As a child grows, he acquires or learns attitudes and behaviour patterns from his parents and other family members. Some of these include personal qualities as work and study habits, moral convictions, neatness or cleanliness, and consideration of others. In the process of growing up children have to learn to adapt to their specific

families. The various types of faulty relationships between a child and his parents are one of the major causes of personality disorders and other mental ailments. (*For details refer to chapter on Causes of Abnormal Behaviour*). However, some individual's with a personality disorders come from families that appear to be stable and healthy. It has been suggested that these individual's are biologically hypersensitive to normal family stress levels. Levels of the brain chemical (neurotransmitter) dopamine may influence an individual's level of novelty seeking, and serotonin levels may influence aggression thus making an otherwise normally developed individual behave in an abnormal manner.

3. **Mass Media**: The media exposes us to a lot of information. Sometimes the information is very dangerous and threatening and at times, it makes a hype of minor issues. When susceptible people are exposed to such information, their anxiety level may go up by an irrationally perceived threat to their being. This anxiety in turn may make them withdraw from society as a precautionary measure. This isolation then may begin to depress them and this chain of symptoms may soon become unending leading to exhibition of abnormal behaviour. However, generally such causes are temporary and short-lived.

TAMING THE DEVIL OF PERSONALITY DISORDERS

1. **Psychotherapy**: As the causes of personality disorders are various so are the treatments for each specific disorder. However, there are some general principles, which apply to all such treatments. Psychotherapy is at the core of care for these various personality disorders. Because personality disorders produce symptoms as a result of poor or limited coping skills, psychotherapy aims to improve perceptions of and responses to social and environmental stressors. It bases itself on the general principle that individual's with personality disorders usually do not see a problem with their own behaviour; hence

they have to be confronted and made aware of the harmful consequences of their maladaptive thoughts and behaviours. Keeping this fact in mind, a therapist repeatedly needs to point out the undesirable consequences of their thought and behaviour patterns. At times, it also becomes essential for the therapist to set limits to which the individual can do a specific behaviour. The support and involvement of the family is also very essential. They have to play an active role in either positively reinforcing required behaviours/thoughts or punishing or diminishing undesired problematic ones. If required the psychiatrist may also prescribe some mild antidepressants. However, in most of the cases of personality disorders there is no need for medication.

2. **Self-Help**: The best way to tame the devil of your personality disorders is to make corrections to your lifestyle. The following simple tips will prove useful if adopted otherwise also.
   - Take regular therapy. Have patience it is not magic which will work overnight. It takes time as well as your commitment. If you cooperate and regularly follow the advice of your therapist, it will do wonders to your personality.
   - Keep yourself physically as well as mentally active. Do regular excises, read, play games, go out, and enjoy life. Be happy and cheerful. In short, activate your happiness.
   - Do not take alcohol or drugs. Quit them if you are consuming either. They end up harming you physically as well as mentally.
   - Make your life simple. Plan and schedule things in such a manner, that it takes the stress off your back. Relax and take up only what you can manage. There is a long life ahead. Stress will only cut it short.
   - Learn how to relax and manage your stress – take some lessons if required. Practise relaxation on a regular basis.
   - Try avoiding those environmental and situational factors,

which are causing you problems – take a break and go for a vacation. A change always does well.

- Sleep well and eat well. Keep your body healthy for a healthy mind to dwell within the same.
- Give vent to your frustrations – express your anger, pain, grief, frustrations by writing them down in a piece of paper. Tear it and throw it in the dustbin because they deserve to be there not within you.
- Socialize. Make friends and move out with them. Avoid isolation – it is depressing.
- Remain focused on your goals – the goal of curing your personality disorder. It your life you make it or break it – the choice is yours.

We should remember that we are the makers and not the slaves of our lives. Let not the past bring despair and hopelessness into out present. Pledge that you can and you will overcome all the hurdles that come your way in shaping a good personality for yourself. Take a step at a time. Rest if you must but do not quit. Nothing is impossible to achieve if we have the will to do so. What it all needs is courage and determination. Where the going gets tough the tough get going. So get moving towards attaining a better mental health.

Chapter 20

The Devils Defenses – Disarm It

"Although defense mechanisms serve a useful protective function, they usually involve some measure of self-deception and reality distortion, and may seriously interfere with the effective resolution of the actual problem. Ego defense mechanisms are considered maladaptive when they become the predominant means of coping with stressors. Ego-defense mechanisms are learned, usually during early childhood. They are developed to deal with inner hurt, pain, anger, anxiety, sadness, and self-devaluation. They operate on relatively automatic and habitual levels."

"In distorting reality, there is a change in perception, which allows for a lessening of anxiety, with a corresponding reduction in felt tension".

When an individual faces such circumstances which give rise to anxiety within him then the ego erects defenses to protect the individual from psychological damage. Sometimes we may be knowingly using these defense mechanisms but largely they occur unconsciously and work to distort reality. This distortion of reality is what ends up being harmful to the individual on many an occasions. However, we cannot say that all the defense mechanisms are unhealthy. Some also help us in adapting to situations and thereby function normally. The problem arises when these defense mechanisms are overused in order to avoid dealing with problems. Table 19.1 shows the various defense mechanisms and their function.

When coping with anxiety filled and stressful situations we are confronted with two problems. The first is to meet the requirements of the situation and secondly to protect ourselves from psychological damage and disorganization. When we feel competent to handle the situation, our behaviour tends to be task–oriented i.e. aimed primarily at dealing with the requirements of the situation in terms of adjustment. However, when we feel inadequate and threatened by the situation we tend to be defense – oriented i.e. we aim primarily at protecting ourselves from hurt and disorganization.

TABLE 19.1

- **Denial of Reality:** Protecting self from unpleasant reality by refusal to perceive it or face it.
- **Fantasy:** Gratifying frustrated desires by imaginary achievements.
- **Repression:** Preventing painful or dangerous thoughts from entering consciousness.
- **Rationalization:** Attempting to prove that one's behaviour is 'rational' and justifiable and thus worthy of self and social approval.
- **Projection:** Placing blame for difficulties upon others or attributing one's own unethical desires to others.
- **Reaction Formation:** Preventing dangerous desires from being expressed by adopting exaggerated opposed attitudes and types of behaviour and using them as 'barriers'.
- **Displacement:** Discharging pent-up feelings, usually hostility, on objects less dangerous than those, which initially aroused the emotion.
- **Emotional Insulation:** Reducing ego involvement and withdrawing into passivity to protect self from hurt.
- **Intellectualization:** Cutting off affective charge from hurtful situations or separating incompatible attitudes by logic-tight compartments.
- **Undoing:** Atoning for and thus counteracting immoral desires or acts.
- **Regression:** Retreating to earlier developmental level involving less mature responses and usually a lower level of aspiration.
- **Identification:** Increasing feelings of worth by identifying self with person or institution of illustrious standing.
- **Introjection:** Incorporating external values and standards into ego structure so individual is not at their mercy as external threats.
- **Compensation:** Covering up weakness by emphasizing desirable trait or making up for frustration in one area by over-gratification in another.

WHICH DEFENSES YOU USE – FIND OUT

This measure is designed to help you evaluate your our adjustive behaviour in terms of handling anxious and stressful situations and know whether you handle them well or not. Read each statement carefully and then assign the "point" (0 - 3) in the blank space provided at the beginning of each statement. *The point you choose to assign is to be based on the frequency with which you display the characteristic traits in the statement.* Kindly note this is only a rough measure developed by me with limited statements for each factor. Ignore the alphabetic signs given while responding.

POINTS

0 - Never.
1 - Sometimes.
2 - Mostly.
3 - Always.

A – (D-D)

_____ 1. I get hostile when frustrated.
_____ 2. I blame others for mistakes made by me.
_____ 3. I take my anger out on others.
_____ 4. I inflict pain on myself when frustrated.
_____ 5. In times of trouble, I think of committing suicide.
_____ **Total**

B – (W-R)

_____ 1. I withdraw myself from frustrating situations.
_____ 2. I imagine I have won my lost battles.
_____ 3. I take a vacation when the going gets tough.
_____ 4. I do not think about anything bad that has happened in the past.
_____ 5. I forget past experiences.
_____ **Total**

C – (W-F)

_____ 1. I dream about having sex with persons I am attracted to.

_____ 2. I have daydreams.

_____ 3. I see myself as a hero in my dreams.

_____ 4. I build castles in the air.

_____ 5. I dream of people admiring me for the courage I have to face my sufferings.

_____ **Total**

D – (W-RG)

_____ 1. I feel like re-living my childhood.

_____ 2. I run away from reality.

_____ 3. I cry very easily.

_____ 4. I display my emotions quickly.

_____ 5. I bite my nails in distress.

_____ **Total**

E – (W-Dr)

_____ 1. I turn away from unpleasant sights.

_____ 2. I refuse to discuss unpleasant topics.

_____ 3. I faint in traumatic situations.

_____ 4. I deny criticism of myself.

_____ 5. In troubled times I loose myself in work.

_____ **Total**

F – (C-S)

_____ 1. I masturbate.

_____ 2. In sad times, I write poetry.

_____ 3. I write down my thoughts.

_____ 4. I sing smutty songs.

_____ 5. I tell dirty stories/jokes.

_____ **Total**

G – (C-Rf)

_____ 1. I love my enemies.

_____ 2. I am orthodox in my thinking.

_____ 3. I am not sexually attracted to good-looking persons.

_____ 4. I act opposite to what I feel.

_____ 5. I show sexual morality in place of proximity.

_____ **Total**

H – (C-Pr)

_____ 1. I blame others for my miseries.
_____ 2. I have a feeling that people dislike me.
_____ 3. I avoid anxiety arousing tasks.
_____ 4. I find my thoughts intolerable.
_____ 5. I am unable to face my inadequacy.
_____ **Total**

I – (C –C)

_____ 1. I compensate for my weaknesses.
_____ 2. I do not venture into things I feel I will fail in.
_____ 3. I disguise my weak traits.
_____ 4. I put forth my best before others.
_____ 5. I try showing myself superior to others.
_____ **Total**

J – (C-I)

_____ 1. I make excuses.
_____ 2. I balance contradictory ideas well.
_____ 3. I reason for the wrongs I do.
_____ 4. I emotionally detach myself from painful situations.
_____ 5. I like whatever I do.
_____ **Total**
_____ **Grand Total (Total of all sections)**

SCORING

After having assigned your points, total them up separately for each section. This is your score for each defense mechanism. After you have done this, add up the total of each section. This will be your total score on this measure.

THE DEFENSES YOU USE – INTERPRETATION OF YOUR SCORES

1. **Displacement [A – (D-D)]**: This represents your score on the mechanism of *displacement*. This is a defense in which we attack unpleasant threatening situations to prevent ourselves from feelings of hurt and anxiety. If you have scored in the

range of 11 – 15 then you have a high displacement score. This means that you have aggressive reactions towards unpleasant happenings in your life and try chasing them away with your aggression, which is aimed generally towards some object or person other than that which is actually causing you frustration. This transfer of hostility is called displacement. The reasons for such a behaviour of yours may be several. You may be afraid to express hostility directly towards the one responsible for your frustrations hence you take it out on some innocent but less threatening person. The most frequent forms of displaced aggression are *scrapegoating, "free-floating" anger,* and *suicide.* Using Displacement as a strategy for handling anxious and stressful situations is not going to make you healthy but in turn make the significant others in your life also unhealthy. It is like adding fuel to the fire of stress and anxiety. Aggression will never ever lead to solving frustrating situations and moods.

2. **Repression [B – (W-R)]**: This represents your score on the mechanism of *repression.* This is a defense by means of which, we try to exclude threatening or painful thoughts and desires from our consciousness. If you have scored in the range of 11 – 15 then you have a high repression score. This means that by using this mechanism you try to escape out of anxious and frustrating situations by forgetting them. However, this has long-term unhealthy consequences. Have you ever had bad dreams? Have you ever been in gloomy moods not knowing reasons? This is how your mental equilibrium is disturbed in the end and very seldom, there is a cure for it. You may have the need to consult a clinical psychologist/psychiatrist if you are tormented beyond explanation and reason. The reasons are that such unpleasant happenings have been deeply repressed by you and forgotten but they actually are still there within you. They are simply cast out of the conscious mind into the unconscious mind. A barrier is constructed against these repressed memories to prevent their re-entry in the field

of your attention – but they do re-enter in disguised forms making you feel sad and unhappy for reasons you do not know. Thus if your score on repression is high you need to learn not to run away from situations but accept and face them boldly. Let the sunset and let there be a new dawn. With time, acceptance will pave a way for better handling of situations and circumstances.

3. **Fantasy [C – (W-F)]**: This represents your score on the mechanism of *fantasy*. If you have scored in the range of 11 – 15, you are high on fantasy. This means that when you feel anxious or frustrated and are not able to attain your desires you retreat into fantasy world. In this world, you seek imaginative satisfaction of your thwarted desires. Have you ever felt sexually attracted to someone and imagined making love with him/her? Have you ever thrashed up your aggressor in your day/night dreams? Have you ever shot some one who insulted or bullied you in your dreams? In addition, many more such dreams and fantasies. There are two common varieties of wish – fulfilling fantasy: *The Conquering Hero* and *The Suffering Hero*. In the previous fantasy, one imagines himself/herself to be a great person in whichever aspect he wants to be thought of. In the latter one, the person imagines himself to be suffering and when, people come to know of his suffering, they praise his courage to bear with it. Do not get worried if your score is high or even low on this mechanism. To create fantasies or daydreams as a temporary escape from the frustrations of reality is a perfectly normal activity. However, watch out that it is not carried so far that you give up striving for *constructive and socially-morally accepted* satisfaction in the real world. This is where your true satisfaction will come from.
4. **Regression [D – (W-Rg)]**: This represents your score on the mechanism of *regression*. Under stressful and threatening situations sometimes a frustrated individual unconsciously seeks to return to an earlier, more secure period of his life.

Check out your score and if it lies in the range of 11 – 15 then you are using this mechanism quite often. You may be fleeing from the painful realities and responsibilities of the present to the protected existence of your childhood. You maybe reverting to old habits of adjustment – such as weeping, sulking, or emotional displays – which worked in the past but are scarcely adequate for solving adult problems. Going back in time never helps – it will only make your happiness history. Think like a man of action, act like a man of thought.

5. **Denial of Reality [E – (W-Dr)]:** This represents your score on the mechanism *denial of reality*. If you have scored in the range of 11 – 15 then you are evading reality most of the time. You maybe turning away from unpleasant sights, refusing to discuss unpleasant topics, faint when confronted with a traumatic situation, deny criticism, or becoming so preoccupied with work that there is no time to deal with marital, child-rearing (if you are married), or other personal problems. You maybe trying to put up an act for self-satisfaction that any unpleasant thing, if happening to you, is actually not happening at all. This denial may bring you temporary peace of mind but it chases away chances of attaining and maintaining a healthy mental life. You will be mentally healthy when what you think, what you say, and what you do are in harmony and reality holds these three together.
6. **Sublimation and Substitution [F – (C-S)]:** This represents your score on the mechanism *sublimation and substitution*. If you have scored in the range of 11 – 15 then you are high on using this mechanism. Whenever you are not able to satisfy any particular need of yours due to reasons ranging from physical inaccessibility or the behaviour involved in achieving your goal seeming to be painful or guilt – provoking, you then tend to resort to indirect means of obtaining gratification by choosing an alternate goal and directing your energies towards the same. Like, for example, when sexually charged, one may use masturbation as an alternative discharge. Such goals never provide exactly the same satisfaction as original goals. They

provide an outlet for the expression of our frustrated desires and often afford real satisfactions of their own. Such indirect expression of a need may take the form of either sublimation or substitution. In *sublimating* a need, which we cannot satisfy directly, we accept some alternative goal which provides a *socially acceptable* outlet of expression and which provides partial satisfactions that are free of guilt feelings. Although the new goal is symbolic of our original one, it can be pursued openly without feelings of guilt. Artistic activities are often interpreted as sublimation. Reading and writing romantic prose and verse are other socially approved sublimations of the sexual drive, even though their sexual element is often rather thinly disguised. According to some psychologists and psychiatrists, all forms of work – science and business as well as fine arts – result from the sublimation of sexual energy. *Sex here means all instinctive, pleasure – seeking impulses of humans*. Frustrated impulses are sometimes expressed indirectly by the *substitution* of activities in which the conscious quality of the desire is not fundamentally changed. When sexual impulses are frustrated, for example, substitution may take the form of masturbation or undesirable verbal behaviour – telling risqué stories, writing obscene poetry, singing smutty songs. Substitution is likely to involve activity that is less socially acceptable than sublimation, so that it is typically accompanied by some feelings of self–disapproval, guilt, and inferiority. The moral of this long mechanism is that these cannot get you satisfaction and assure you a good mental health if you rely on them for too long.

7. **Reaction Formation [G – (C-Rf)]**: This is your score on the mechanism known as *reaction formation*. If you have scored in the range of 11 – 15 then you are high on using this mechanism. People using this defense pattern are born real life actors. They act just the opposite of their thinking and thus escape out of dangerous desires. If high on this, you may be portraying love in place of hatred, sexual morality in place of sexual promiscuity and its likes. In this way, you are erecting

obstacles or barriers that reinforce your repression and keep your real desires and feelings from conscious awareness and from being carried out overtly. Have you heard the story about an unmarried woman who looked hopefully under her bed each night for fear that a man may be lurking there! Though this mechanism may help in maintaining socially approved behaviour and avoid awareness of threatening and self–devaluating desires but because it is self–deceptive, and not subject to conscious control. It often results in exaggerated and rigid fears or beliefs that may complicate one's adjustive reactions and lead to excessive harshness or severity in dealing with the lapses of others. Thus, it can result in behaviour that is personally and socially harmful – bringing in more pain and agony.

8. **Projection [H – (C-Pr)]**: This is your score on the mechanism of *projection.* If you have scored in the range of 11 – 15 then you are using this mechanism for seeking happiness in coping with unhappy situations. It maybe that at times when you find your true thoughts and feelings intolerable, then you not only must be repressing them but also trying to convince yourself unconsciously that other people have these thoughts and feelings towards you as well. Using this mechanism, individuals direct their aggressive feelings towards others rather than towards themselves. Projection also enables a person to blame other people – or even things – for failures that are essentially their own making. Such individuals make poor discrimination a form of avoidance for unhappy situations. They not only discriminate, that an error has occurred due to their own carelessness rather than that of the other, but they also avoid unpleasant experience of facing up to their own inadequate performance. Running away from facts and blaming others never helps in the solution of any problem. In fact, it causes more gloom because in the hearts of hearts one knows what the realities are. One should learn to bravely stand up for the truth and accept what life is on an as- is- where-is basis.

9. **Compensation [I – (C –C)]**: If you have scored in the range of 11 – 15 then you are high on using the mechanism of *compensation*. The feelings of inferiority that typically accompany failure in some activity are often counter–balanced by the individual's entering some other sphere of activity in which he can succeed. That is, he "covers up" his felt weaknesses by withdrawing from situations in which he would be evident and turns instead to activities more likely to bring success and approval. While *compensating* an individual attempts to disguise the presence of a weak or undesirable trait by emphasizing a desirable one. This compensatory behaviour is aimed at bringing social approval to the individual; it also sometimes results in accomplishments of considerable social value. Compensation may look positively oriented but such activities, like any other defense mechanism, ceases to be of value to an individual when it gets out of control. For example a person who is not good looking may try being over assertive by "showing off" in many ways which may not be realistic. Such individuals often develop a deep sense of inferiority that ordinary acceptance is no longer sufficient to relieve it – to feel safe and secure he must keep trying to prove that he is *superior* to others. In the end, this *overcompensation* is seldom effective in reducing frustration, since the social disapproval incurred by such behaviour only tends to increase the individual's sense of failure and inferiority. Thus, compensation also is not a ticket to good mental health.
10. **Intellectualization [J-(C-I)]**: Another way of compromise with problems is to intellectualize them, thus partially divesting them of personal significance or painful feeling. This mechanism is a combination of three basic mechanisms labelled *intellectualization*. The three basic mechanisms of intellectualization are (1) *Rationalization or excuse-making;* (2) *Isolation or the use of "logic–tight compartments"*; (3) *Undoing or ritualistic "cleansing" behaviour*. Check your score and if you have scored in the range of 11 – 15 then

you are high on this mechanism as a whole. Rationalization is an unconscious process of devising seemingly logical explanations for a situation that would result in loss of social approval or self–esteem. It takes many forms. There is the "sour grapes" attitude. There is the jilted lover who suddenly realizes that his former girl had certain flaws and there is this well sold philosophy of happiness, which says, "Not in doing what you like, but in liking what you do is the secret of happiness". In addition, there is the rationalization of the wrongdoer, who claims noble motivation to justify an act, which is anything but noble. Although rationalizations are "logical", they are generally based on false premises. Most of our everyday rationalizations are inconsequential, but if we start relying too much on them we may develop unrealistic ways of dealing with life. Good mental health can only be attained and maintained through realistic thought and action.

11. **Isolation**: We sometimes also may be in a habit of trying to avoid conflict between two opposing desires or attitudes by keeping them apart in consciousness. Certain ideas are sealed off in mental compartments, as it were, and allowed to function in isolation from conflicting ones. Thus, we never have to choose between them. This is *isolation.* Such mental compartments are said to be "logic tight" because they enable the individual to maintain contradictory ideas and attitudes at the conscious level without recognizing that they are logically incompatible. People with logic–tight compartments think and act inconsistently and inconsistency never leads one to have a healthy mind.
12. **Undoing**: This is a mechanism whereby an individual can divest himself of painful feelings by ritualistic "cleaning". We try to wash away our sins and clear our conscience by doing many ritualistic acts. If only the Holy Waters and other such things could clean our conscience this world would be just too full with happy people – water – water everywhere and not a soul of sin!

INTERPRETATION OF THE TOTAL SCORE

If your total score lies in the range of 113 – 150 then you are *extremely high* on using a combination of the various defense mechanisms stated above and this is not a healthy sign for your overall well-being. If your total score lies, in the range of 76 - 112, you are *high* on using a combination of the various defense mechanisms and you need to watch out. If your total score lies, in the range of 38 – 75 you are in the *moderate zone* and need not worry since most of us lie in that range. If your total score lies, in the range of 0 – 37 you are surely a mentally healthy individual, well-adjusted with his surroundings and who has adopted proper coping strategies.

Conclusion: *The use of defense mechanisms is not in itself a sign of unhealthy practice. Whether use of these mechanisms is healthy or unhealthy depends largely upon how much we rely on them and how well they actually reduce our stresses, anxieties and other psychological problems. We all use these mechanisms from time to time and if used sparingly and without cost of others, they are nothing to worry about. If they allow us to feel more comfortable, as they often do their value in reducing tension and letting us get on with important problems more than offsets the trivial self–deceptions they entail. However, if a person comes to depend on them too much, then these defensive patterns may be harmful. They do not solve real problems; they only relieve anxiety about it.*

It is thus important for us to become aware about which defense mechanism we are using and to what extent, so that we can assess our behaviour more rationally and come to terms with the unknown side of ourselves. I assure you that by this awareness program you are going to light the unending flame of good mental health in your life. A flame, which, though will burn forever, yet needs to be protected from strong winds and rains of life's realities through acceptance of facts. Good mental health comes from courage to accept the things we cannot change, strength to change those, which we can, and above all the wisdom to know the difference.

Chapter 21

Taming The Devils – Angelic Interventions

"Psychotherapy or personal counselling with a psychotherapist, is an intentional interpersonal relationship used by trained psychotherapists to aid a client or patient in problems of living. It aims to increase the individual's sense of their own well-being. Psychotherapists employ a range of techniques based on experiential relationship building, dialogue, communication and behaviour change and that are designed to improve the mental health of a client or patient, or to improve group relationships".

"The principle aim of psychotherapy is not to transport one to an impossible state of happiness, but to help the client acquire steadfastness and patience in the face of suffering."

To have control over our body and mind sometimes we need help of a professionally trained paramedical or medical practitioner. The people who can help us in our psychological distress are psychiatrists, clinical psychologists, psychiatric social workers, and counsellors. Visiting either one of them for the solution of your mental health problems does not attach any stigma to your name in society. In fact, not visiting them does attach one. It is important that you know about then as well before you seek help for your psychological problems from them. In addition, you should be aware about the various intervention programs, which can help you overcome your problems.

WHO PRACTISES PSYCHOTHERAPY?

In India, practitioners of psychotherapy can be divided into four groups, largely based on the type of training they undergo. The type of training is also likely to have a strong influence on the model used by a particular therapist.

1. **Psychiatrists**: They are the only one in the four groups that have an M.D. degree. They are only legally permitted to prescribe psychoactive drugs that affect the way their patients feel and think, and consequently, the way they behave. They are also the only therapists permitted to prescribe electroshock treatment.

2. **Clinical Psychologists**: They do either an M.Phil. in clinical psychology from a recognized institute and thereafter some obtain a doctorate degree in the area of clinical psychology. Their training includes laboratory work, research designs, and specialized training in abnormal behaviour and therapy techniques, usually followed by an internship in which they work with clients (mental patients) under professional supervision.
3. **Psychiatric Social Workers**: They study for two years to earn a master's degree in psychiatric social work, including a year's internship in social work.
4. **Counselling Psychologists and Counsellors**: They earn their postgraduate degree in psychology and thereafter peruse a one-year diploma course in counselling and guidance from a recognized institute. They do their internship in a counselling setting. Often their training and attention is concentrated on specific areas such as student, marriage, or family counselling. Often their practice focuses on problems in adjustment rather than abnormal functioning.

WHAT IS PSYCHOTHERAPY?

Psychotherapy literally means "*mental treatment*". It is a term applied to the treatment of personality and behaviour disorders by psychological methods of therapy – in contrast to physical methods such as drugs and surgery. Psychotherapy can best be described as a set of procedures by which the psychotherapist uses language to change the life of the client (patient). In psychotherapy, change is the key element. This change may be cognitive, behavioural, or emotional – that is, therapy may change the way a person thinks, behaves, or feels – or all of these.

The fundamental objective of all psychotherapy, regardless of the techniques employed, is to help the individual improve his modes of response to real life situations. To accomplish this end, psychotherapy does much more than give the client intellectual insight into his personality problems. It tries to help him improve his emotional responses, his way of handling difficulties, and his ability to meet his fundamental needs.

TYPES OF PSYCHOTHERAPIES

THE PSYCHOANALYTICAL MODEL OF THERAPY

The psychoanalytic model initiated by Freud, locates the origin of abnormal functioning in emotionally painful situations or events experienced in childhood that have resulted in arrested personality development. The patient is thus unable to resolve unconscious conflicts and impulses except by maladaptive defense mechanisms such as excessive repression – we forget and then forget what we forgot.

Psychoanalysis is based on verbal techniques. Its basic problem is to solve psychological problems by bringing the unconscious conflicts into the conscious mind, where they may be confronted and resolved by the person. The focus is on feelings rather than on behaviour. Psychoanalysis aims to change the patient's entire life-style and personality rather than just certain behaviours. In Freudian terms, psychoanalysis is designed to strengthen the ego, increase the awareness of the id, and bring the superego under control.

Psychoanalysis is usually an involved process that takes years to complete. The role of the psychoanalyst is largely passive; it is that of a guide and interpreter rather than a teacher. One of the major problems the analyst must deal with is the emotional resistance of the patient to the painful awareness that an emotional problem exists. Therefore, analysis must do more than uncover the emotional origins of problems, if effective therapy is to take place, it must enable the person to acknowledge and confront these problems.

Techniques of Psychoanalysis

- **Free Association**: Psychoanalysis uses many techniques—most of them originated by Freud—as part of the therapeutic process. One of the best known is free association, in which the patient is encouraged to say whatever thought comes to mind, regardless of how illogical, irrelevant, or embarrassing they seem. Freud said that free association should be like someone viewing scenes from a train window, smoothly flowing by. The theory is that by disregarding intellectual judgment and interpretation, the person will bypass the ego's defenses and produce clues to the unconscious source of the problems. Of course, it rarely happens this easily. What gets in the way is the person's own resistance, which occurs in the form of blanks, obviously contrived association, or disputes with the therapist. The form or source of this resistance is regarded as significant by the psychoanalyst and a possible opportunity for insight and interpretation, because it is a clue that the person is getting close to the source of a problem.

- **Interpretation**: This is another key technique used by the psychoanalyst to make the unconscious conscious, to bring hidden emotions to the surface. When the person seems ready to face underlying problems, the analyst suggests possible hidden meanings or defense mechanisms revealed by the person's actions or statements. The analyst points out connections and associations the person may not have seen—connections between belief and actions or between current attitudes and something that happened in the past. The person may deny these connections or use them to gain insight into the unconscious source of the problem.

In addition to interpreting a person's resistance, psychoanalysts also interpret the person's dreams. Freud called dreams the "royal road to unconscious". By interpreting dreams, the psychoanalyst tries to help people recognize unconscious impulses that are threatening to them.

As psychoanalysis progresses, a special relationship, called transference, begins to develop between patient and analyst. Patients begin to form irrational emotional expectations of the analyst. According to Freud, these unrealistic interpretations are a result of transferring past relationships with important adults onto the analyst, relating to the analyst as if he or she were the parent figure. Although this transference is unconscious, patients expect the analyst to react the way their parents would, so they can re-enact repressed wishes and experiments.

THE LEARNING MODEL OF THERAPY

The learning model sees abnormal functioning as patterns of behaviour that are learned by the individual - "bad habits". Thus, the learning approach to psychotherapy involves extinguishing the maladaptive patterns and learning ones that are more appropriate. The extinction and learning follow the principles of classical conditioning, and modeling.

Therapy is centered on the problem behaviours themselves; there is no attempt to work back to their origin in the person's childhood. Thus, most learning therapy approaches come under the behavioural therapy. The first step in behavioural therapy is to define the problem in terms of measurable behaviour. Behavioural therapists are not content with description of feeling or undefined fears. Once the specific behaviours in need of change are defined, treatment programs using conditioning techniques are worked out. In this way, the therapist adapts the method used to the particular problem, rather than using the same method for all problems.

Types of Learning Model of Therapy

Systematic Desensitization: Behavioural approaches have been applied quite often to problems of anxiety and neurosis. Systematic desensitization is based on the principle of reciprocal inhibition, in which the person substitutes for the undesired response a response that is incompatible or competitive with it. For example, anxiety responses may be extinguished by gradually associating the anxiety situation or stimulus with a relaxation response.

First, the person is trained in relaxation techniques over a period of several sessions and homework assignments. The next step is to make up a hierarchy in which various aspects of the anxiety-producing situation are ranked from extremely mild to extremely tense and anxiety filled. The client is asked to relax and then to experience or imagine each step in the hierarchy, starting at the lower or mild end.

Through repeated short exposures while using relaxation technique, the person learns to imagine each step without feelings of anxiety. As each step in the hierarchy is "conquered", the person moves on until he or she can experience or imagine the highest level, which used to be the most disturbing, without anxiety. The final step is for the person to carry the learned relaxed responses into the critical environment.

In order for systematic desensitization to work, it is obviously necessary that people be able to identify what they are afraid of. For this reason, the approach has been most successfully applied to phobias and anxieties that can be broken down into basic elements.

Systematic desensitization includes two central ingredients: a gradual hierarchy of fears and relaxation training. Therapists who use this approach argue that the experience of fearful stimuli by themselves - without the relaxation training - will only intensify anxiety. The implosive therapists argue just the opposite.

Implosive Therapy: In this type of behavioural therapy, people are instructed to tackle an undesirable behaviour head on by imagining themselves in the worst anxiety-producing situation for long periods. Rather than easing the anxiety, the therapist attempts to increase it by adding frightening details to the imagined scene. The theory is that prolonged exposure to the anxiety-producing stimulus in the absence of reinforcement defuses its power.

Aversion Counterconditioning: With some problems, rather than getting rid of a negative response, it is thought to be helpful to develop one. Undesirable habits such as smoking, overeating, or excessive drinking are hard for many persons to break. The behavioural approach of aversive counter-conditioning seeks to help people to extinguish their excessive attraction to smoking, food, or alcohol by associating a negative reaction, such as nausea or anxiety, with the same stimulus.

The undesirable attraction to the object is extinguished by repeatedly paring it with an unpleasant consequence such as verbal ridicule, nausea-producing drugs, or electric shock. For example, a chronic overeater is repeatedly offered a large serving of a favourite food, and then given a mild electric shock with each bite. Thus, in conditioning terms, the attractive stimulus, the food, is the conditioned stimulus; it is paired with the unattractive stimulus, the shock, which is the unconditioned stimulus. This pairing produces a fear or revulsion response. When the food comes to elicit fear, its attraction no longer exists—the food is no longer tempting. It is, important, to replace the overeating with a more desirable response that is somehow fulfilling or tension releasing. Otherwise, relapse rates in this kind of treatment are high.

Operant Conditioning Therapies: Operant approaches to therapy follow the notion that you can shape desired behaviours by rewarding them and by not rewarding undesirable alternative behaviours. One of the best-known operant conditioning therapies is the token economy programs. This approach has been used with many problems as schizophrenic disorders, retardation, and school misbehaviour and has had some success in problems typically resistant to change.

Token-economy programs are often practised in controlled environments such as mental hospitals or psychiatric wards. Positive behaviour is reinforced by the reward of tokens that can be exchanged later for special privileges. Thus, behaviour is reinforced right away by the token. The therapist controls what and when the token is traded for. It is a simple system, which has a big advantage—even severely retarded children quickly catch on to the use of tokens.

The therapist and sometimes the patient as well, controls the choice of specific behaviour that are to be reinforced and the items or privileges for which the token may be exchanged. An advantage of using tokens is that with one item you can reinforce many different people having many different needs or desires.

With the token-economy programs, the therapist can also shape behaviour. This has the advantage that the therapist can start with the behaviour the person is already demonstrating. Thus, the token-economy approach is good with very apathetic or with drawn patients, who are not likely to spontaneously show the final, desired behaviour. Remarkable results have been claimed for token-economy programs in improving behaviour with institutions. It is not essential that an operant approach actually use tokens, a more direct means of reinforcement can be used as well.

Modeling: Another behavioural approach is modeling. In this relatively new technique, a person who fears a certain object repeatedly observes another person—the model—interacting with the object. For example, a person who fears snakes watches a model handling a snake. After the observer sees that the model survives the experience with no bad consequences, he or she comes to believe that there is no basis for an anxiety response. This is a kind of social learning. The person learns something by observing rather than by experiencing it directly.

Modeling is very effective in overcoming neurotic fears because it gives the person a chance to see someone else go through the anxiety-producing situation without getting hurt. Usually neurotic people avoid these situations and therefore never learn that they will not hurt them.

Modeling is also used in programs for people with psychotic patterns of functioning to teach them the social skills they have never had a chance to learn. In this sort of programs therapists model appropriate behaviour and set up group situations in which patients play different roles with the therapist watching and coaching.

THE BIOLOGICAL MODEL OF THERAPY

According to the biological model, abnormal behaviour is caused by a malfunction of the body. Treatment is therefore designed to make a particular change in the person's biological functioning. This may be done through such means as drugs, electroshock therapy, or psychosurgery.

Types of Biological Model of Therapy

Chemotherapy: Chemotherapy, the treatment of abnormal behaviour with drugs, is the most widespread biological technique. The drugs used in chemotherapy can be classified as antianxiety, antidepressant, or antipsychotic. As their names apply, each type of drug is aimed at treating a specific area of abnormal functioning. The treatment of anxiety and neurotic problems with antianxiety drugs is widely practised not only by therapists, but also by medical doctors who give their patients something to "calm their nerves" and by individuals who swallow a tranquillizer whenever they feel emotionally upset. The popularity of these drugs is due, in large part, to the speed with which they work. When they do work, they seem almost to be an instant cure. The "instant cure" however, may be little more than a temporary alleviation of symptoms. There is growing evidence that the so-called tranquillizers, such as Librium, Miltown, and Valium, are physically and psychologically addictive when used continuously in high dosages over a long period. They are also dangerous, at times fatal, and even more addictive when used with alcohol. Some people experience uncomfortable and sometimes serious side effects that must be dealt with, such as tremors and problems in motor control. Moreover, those people who have improved on these drugs, and have been released from hospitals often show high readmission rates. This has led to what is often called the "revolving door syndrome"- patients improve enough to be released, but they are not capable of coping with the outside world. Some stop taking their medication and the symptoms recur; others simply do not have the social or vocational skills to cope outside the institutions.

Thus, these drugs cannot be said to be a "cure". The real value of drugs lies in the fact that it brings patients to the point where more traditional forms of psychotherapy are possible. Thus, while further clarification and improvement are needed, these medication have already made significant progress in the treatment of schizophrenia, where before the progress was very poor.

Electroshock Treatment: One of the most controversial biological treatments is electroshock. It is usually used only with people for whom other forms of therapy have not been effective. Therapists have resorted to it less frequently since the antidepressant drugs became available. The basic procedure is to pass a brief electric current of about 100 volts through the brain by means of electrodes placed on either side of the forehead. The result of the shock is a convulsive seizure that lasts for about a minute, following which the person loses consciousness for several minutes. The treatment is often accompanied by a memory loss of unpredictable length, ranging from a few minutes to several hours, along with some more lingering memory difficulties. Before receiving electroshock today, people are given a sedative and a muscle relaxant, which reduce the risk of injury and seems to minimize the discomfort. Most people receive 6-9 treatments at the rate of 3-4 week.

Although electroshock apparently reduces symptoms in many cases of depression, no one knows for sure how or why it works. Some experimenters think that it temporarily stimulates the synthesis of norepinephrine in the brain. Unfortunately, it is not a final cure-the depression often recurs later on.

Psychosurgery: Psychosurgery is easily the most controversial. The prefrontal lobotomy has been particularly controversial. This brain surgery was based on the notion that the frontal lobes of the brain strengthen or increase emotional response, which arise in the thalamus and hypothalamus. Thus, it was thought that cutting the connections between the frontal lobes and these other brain regions would help in many problems as schizophrenia and depression. In the 1940 and 1950, an enormous number of lobotomies were performed with claims of great success. However, subsequent research found that people who have had lobotomies showed very bad side effect, such as seizures, stupor, and extreme listlessness, to say nothing of impaired mental functioning. The Noble Prize- winning procedure fell into disfavour as it became evident that its side effects represented a very significant and serious problem. Thus because of the lobotomy lesson, as well as the success of the relatively less severe medication approaches, psychosurgery today is an experimental and less used approach.

THE HUMANISTIC – EXISTENTIAL MODEL OF THERAPY

For humanistic-existential psychologists, abnormal functioning results from a failure to reach or strive towards ones full potential. In humanistic theories, this is often called a failure to self-actualize; that is, a failure to move towards the fulfillment of one's natural potential as a human being and to be in close touch with who one is, how one feels, and what one actually thinks. In existential theories, too, abnormality represents a failure to reach one's full potential, but this failure is rooted in one's inability to overcome the sources of anxiety built into the existential situation of life, an inability to meet life assertively and give it meaning and take responsibility of one's life. Both theories define abnormal functioning as a failure to be and fulfill oneself and the humanistic-existential approach to therapy seeks to help people get in touch with their real selves, and then make deliberate choices regarding their lives and behaviours, rather than letting outside events determine their behaviour. Years ago, humanistic form of therapy mainly involved some forms of careful and intense self-examination. In recent years, the search for fulfilling one's potential has also used altered states of consciousness such as meditation or yoga.

Types of Humanistic – Existential Model of Therapy

Client – Centered Therapy: The idea underlying client-centered therapy is that therapy must create a totally non-threatening atmosphere in which people can honestly look at, accept themselves, and make relevant decisions. More accurate self-awareness and acceptance will in turn lead to the more functional and productive life-style of self-actualization. Thus, the humanistic technique allows the client a large role in directing the course of the therapy. For therapy to be effective, the client must perceive the therapist as showing unconditional positive regard, empathy, and genuineness. Unconditional positive regard is essential to the concept of client-centered therapy. The therapist must consider the client a worthy human being, without qualification. No judgments should be passed, either against or in support of the client's viewpoint or actions. The therapist must however, show a deep faith in the ability of the client to discover the right path to follow. Because of this unconditional positive regard when clients reveal bizarre or seemingly terrible thoughts, and are still accepted by their therapists, they begin to accept themselves.

Unlike psychoanalysis, in which the therapist attempts to observe and analyze the patient's conception of reality, the client-centered therapist empathizes with the client's world by trying to enter it and experience it from the same viewpoint as the client. When listening to their clients, therapists make remarks reflecting the emotional content of what is being said. They do this to make sure what they are saying, or the implications of what they are saying. This has been described as mirroring client's feelings so that they will see all that is there.

Genuineness means that the therapist must establish a human-to-human relationship with the client, not one that could be interpreted by the client as doctor-patient, expert-amateur, or savior-sinner. The therapist must feel a genuine concern and empathy for the client in order for therapy to be effective.

Gestalt Therapy: Another humanistic approach is Gestalt therapy. It is based on the assumption that all people are innately good. Abnormal functioning originates in the denial of this goodness and the blocking of this expression. Ordinarily, in whatever we perceive, whether it is ideas, events, or emotions, we concentrate on only part of our whole experience: we focus on the figure, or foreground, and largely ignore the background against which the figure appears. According to this therapy, people should perceive the wholeness, or Gestalt, of their experiences.

The purpose of Gestalt therapy is to help people become aware of this wholeness by bringing more of the background into the foreground experience. Great importance is placed on the here and now and that nothing else exists or existed. Therapy encourages the people to recognize the immediate experience in its entirety, which means knowing what they are feeling as well as thinking, so that their behaviour is in harmony with their whole being. To achieve this goal, they must free themselves from trying to live up to the expectations of others. They must be responsible for their own behaviour and recognize their capabilities for self-improvement.

Among the techniques practised by Gestalt therapists, role-playing and projection are used to bring out problems caused by expectations or rules of behaviour that were originally applied by parents and other authority figures and that people have internalized. The purpose is to show that these problems are self-imposed, that they do not result from universal rules that everyone must follow.

Another Gestalt technique is to ask clients to act out the opposite of what they feel. People who feel emotionally unresponsive, for example, would be instructed to react as if they were extremely sensitive and emotionally uninhibited. Through this exercise, clients discover a very real part of their being that had never been allowed open expression. Throughout Gestalt therapy, an effort is made to experience feelings, to acknowledge them, and then work towards changing them if necessary. Gestalt concentrates on the present and how people are now, encouraging them to accept themselves as they are and not as they think they should be.

THE COGNITIVE MODEL OF THERAPY

Cognitive therapies start with the assumption that emotional upsets or abnormal patterns of behaviour result not from what we feel but from what we think (content) or how we think (process). Even if the problem appears to be one of emotion, behaviour, or circumstance, our cognitive mediation (our thoughts) plays the most important role. Thus, cognitive theorists are less concerned with the symptoms than with the thinking process that led to them, and they try to change these thoughts or thinking process in therapy. The cognitive therapies that are best known are of Albert Ellis and Aaron Beck.

Types of Cognitive Model of Therapy

Ellis: Rational Emotive Therapy (RET): Ellis's rational-emotive therapy (RET) focuses primarily on thought content that is, on specific irrational thoughts or assumptions that Ellis says lie at the core of abnormal functioning. This approach, which has been most often applied to problems in anxiety and neurotic functioning, argues that therapy should be directed at pointing out the false beliefs that neurotic persons hold and that lead to their feelings of anxiety. Some of the more common false beliefs at the root of abnormal functioning are the following:

- I must be loved or approved of by virtually every significant other person around me.
- I must be thoroughly competent, adequate, and achieving in all possible respects or I cannot consider myself worthwhile.
- Certain people are bad, wicked, or villainous ...they should be severely punished for it.
- It is awful and catastrophic when things are not the way I want them to be.
- Rational-emotive therapy tries to show the client how to separate rational from irrational thoughts and accept reality. Ellis emphasizes tolerance of oneself, of others, and of inevitable frustration in the real world. Instead of irrationally thinking "I ought to succeed" or "I must succeed", the client learns to accept the rational thought, "it would be better to succeed", or "I may fail in this one thing but that doesn't mean I am a total failure".

This requires, in many cases, big changes in one's basic values and beliefs. In leading clients to this change, RET therapists tend to be much more active than therapists of some other approaches. Unlike client-centered therapy, for example in RET therapists openly challenge statements that they consider irrational. They do not wait for clients to discover irrationality on their own. They give their own personal opinion when asked by clients, and often when not asked. Instead of occasionally interpreting something, like psychoanalysts, or restating, like client-centered therapists, they spend a good deal of time telling their clients the way things are and what is wrong with their thinking.

Among the techniques used by RET therapists are role-playing and modeling. Both of these techniques may be used in individual sessions or in groups to show clients in what ways their thinking is unrealistic and what the consequences of this irrationality are for their relationships with others and their own self-perceptions. RET therapists also try to show unconditional acceptance of their clients. Unlike client-centered therapists, who strive to give unconditional acceptance in a non-judgmental way, RET therapists will criticize their clients for faulty thinking but still demonstrate that they accept them unconditionally even with their flaws. Furthermore, the therapists point out, clients can learn to accept themselves in the same unconditional way.

At this point, RET is one of the most widely practised forms of treatment. RET therapists claim that their techniques not only work faster than therapies that emphasize insight, but that they are more effective in relieving anxiety as well.

Beck's Cognitive Therapy: This therapy has been most often applied to the problems of depression. It traces depressed patterns to both problematic thoughts and distorted thinking processes. It argues that depressed persons have basic "rules", not unlike Ellis's irrational thoughts or assumptions, which underlie their depression. For example, "It would be terrible if someone else had a low opinion of me", or "anything less than total success would be a disaster". While Beck does not describe these rules as irrational, he does see them as very limiting because of their arbitrary, extreme, and unyielding nature. These rules give rise to "automatic thoughts" - negative self-verbalizations that pop into a person's head continually throughout the day.

As well as problematic thoughts, Beck is concerned with distorted thinking processes, which, he says, characterize depressed functioning. These distortions in thinking include jumping to conclusions without having enough evidence and over generalizing from a single event. Usually these distorted thinking processes help to lock in a negative self-view and view of the future.

Beck's cognitive therapy seeks to reveal and change these rules, automatic thoughts, and distorted thinking process. Therapy begins with some tasks that lead the person to experience the joy of success—a pleasure that typically escapes very depressed people. People are assigned a series of tasks within their range of ability. As the person's mood becomes somewhat more elevated in the face of undeniable success, the therapy becomes more cognitive. Clients are helped to recognize and even record their automatic thoughts. They are taught to evaluate and challenge these thoughts rather than accept them automatically. Through a series of cognitive maneuvers, the person comes to further identify and challenge the rules and style of thinking attached to these automatic thoughts.

The treatment program is expected to significantly improve depressed clients in 20 1-hour sessions. Research suggests that Beck's cognitive viewpoint of depression has its merits and that this cognitive form of psychotherapy significantly reduces depression and even compares well to the treatment effectiveness of antidepressant medications.

BIOFEEDBACK

Biofeedback training is an approach that has gained notice recently. The idea behind this approach is that anxiety and other discomforts will be lessened if a person can learn to control the bodily responses involved. Experiments have shown that when subjects are given biofeedback of their present bodily states in the form of audible tones, moving graphs or dials, they can in turn learn to control such bodily reactions as brain-wave pattern, blood pressure, and muscle tension. Since heart rate normally increases as a reaction to fear, for example, people who can be taught to control their heart rate can control fear.

The biofeedback approach has been most successfully applied as an adjunct to treatment for chronic headaches. Providing people who suffer from headaches with feedback and teaching them to control such things, as muscle tension in the forehead region and blood flow in the cranial arteries has proved effective in many cases.

Clearly, the biofeedback approach cuts across the biological, learning, and humanistic models. The biological perspective is represented by the focus on the bodily functions as the center of the problem. The learning approach is at the heart of the training programs in which direct control over involuntary processes is learned by observations and feedback. Biofeedback training's function as a technique that enables people to get in touch with hidden dimensions of themselves and their environments has sometimes led to its classification as a humanistic approach.

GROUP THERAPY

A format whose popularity has grown in the past few decades is "group therapy"' in which several clients simultaneously meet with a therapist. Obviously, such a format is an efficient use of the therapist's time and is usually cheaper for the clients. Moreover, group therapy formats seem to have certain therapeutic advantages over individual therapy. It is sometimes easier to observe oneself by looking at and listening to others. For another, people whose problems have a distinct interpersonal dimension often find the group setting the ideal place to develop the interpersonal skills, perspective, and feelings of relaxation they surely need. Groups vary in several ways. First, they differ in membership and make-up. For example, many groups consist of strangers whose problems have something in common. In other group formats, such as the increasingly popular family therapy or couple therapy groups, the members are hardly strangers.

FAMILY THERAPY

Family therapy brings all the family members together to work on such issues as communication and interaction. As members become better able to relate to one another, the problems of the family and of the individual member should improve significantly. This approach has been particularly helpful in dealing with the problems of children. Working with children alone has often led to only limited success. However, working with them along with their parents and siblings apparently enables a therapist to deal with children's problems in a more comprehensive and successful way. Obviously, working with families, with their many problems and channels of interaction, can be a complex task, and family therapists receive special training in family psychotherapy.

Chapter 22

Giving The Devil His Due – Relax It

The body and mind can heal itself given the right conditions. Relaxation therapy restores harmony and helps to create these conditions for optimum living. It is the releasing of physical and mental tensions. Some people need help and training to understand how to release the physical and mental tensions. Relaxation therapy has a range of techniques to create a profound level of relaxation and through them, into an enhanced psychological integration.

"The time to relax is when you don't have time for it."

The man who doesn't relax and hoot a few hoots voluntarily, now and then, is in great danger of hooting hoots and standing on his head for the edification of the pathologist and trained nurse, a little later on. Thus to have a good physical and mental health it is very important to relax and relaxation therapy through its various techniques helps you do so efficiently.

Relaxation therapy focuses on a combination of breathing and muscle relaxation which aims at giving rest and comfort to the mind, muscles and organs of the body and also many times to treat some medical conditions. Relaxation therapy techniques may include visualization, meditation, water therapy, massage therapy, focused breathing, and muscle relaxing. These various types of techniques provides the body the much needed rest as well as exercise necessary for the maintenance of good physical and mental health. These relaxation techniques though can be employed without the help of a professional trainer but it is still advisable to first learn their basics from a professional.

RELAXATION THERAPY: ITS BENEFITS

Relaxation therapy techniques provide many benefits for people suffering from stress, anxiety disorders, emotional disorders or other medical conditions. Some of those benefits are reduced stress; reduced anxiety; reduced depression; increased ability to deal with emotional problems and stressful situations; decreased panic attacks; increased ability to handle pain; decreased pain; improved breathing and improved sleep.

RELAXATION THERAPY: HOW DOES IT WORK?

The basis of relaxation therapy is to provide relaxation to the body and mind. Relaxation of the body helps in diminishing the pain and physical problems. Mind relaxation lowers the anxiety levels, diminishes stress, and aids in the control of negative emotions, which may be underlying causes of serious psychological disorders. The modus operandi of relaxation therapy is simple. Through relaxation exercises, the individual is trained to focus his thought on things other than those, which are the source of his problems. This in turn relaxes the mind. However, there are also chances that this relaxed state may last only during the period the individual is undergoing the therapy. It is thus also important for the individual to gain insight into his problems and develop his coping abilities to deal with his anxiety, stress, or any other problems he is facing. This can be achieved by combining relaxation therapy with other forms of advisable psychotherapy.

DIFFERENT TYPES OF RELAXATION TECHNIQUES: TRY THEM

There are hosts of different relaxation techniques being sold in the market today to buyers who will pay anything to get relieved from their problems. However, the problem is this that such buyers though can afford to pay the high cost for them but cannot afford to spend adequate time doing simple relaxation on a regular basis. All the body needs is some rest to rejuvenate. It needs to be free for a while from stress and remain in tranquility. There is no other simpler low cost relaxation technique but still unaffordable in terms of time.

Apart from the above simple relaxation technique there are specific techniques depending upon the nature of the problem. Relaxation techniques are also dependent upon personal preferences and considerations. It is best to use those techniques you feel comfortable to use. Thus, before beginning any relaxation training program these minor facts must be kept in mind in order to achieve the maximum benefits. Some of the most popular relaxation techniques are as follows:

PROGRESSIVE MUSCLE RELAXATION

This type of relaxation involves the tensing and then relaxing muscle groups. It is but obvious that it is useful for relaxing the body when there is muscular tension. The idea behind progressive muscle relaxation is that you tense up a group of muscles so that they are as tightly contracted as possible. Hold them in a state of extreme tension for a few seconds. Then, relax the muscles to their previous state. Finally, consciously relax the muscles even further so that you are as relaxed as possible. By tensing your muscles first, you will probably find that you are able to relax your muscles more than would be the case if you tried to relax your muscles directly. Experiment first with progressive muscle relaxation by forming a fist, and clenching your hand as tight as you can for a few seconds. Then relax your hand to its previous tension, and then consciously relax it again so that it is as loose as possible. You should feel deep relaxation in your hand muscles. For maximum relaxation, you can use progressive muscle relaxation in conjunction with breathing techniques and imagery.

This process of relaxation is guaranteed to happen because it is based on a principle of muscle physiology. Whenever you create tension in a muscle and then release the tension the muscle has to relax. The muscle does not have a choice. It must happen. The interesting aspect of this process is that the muscle will not only quickly relax back to its pre-tensed state, but if it is allowed to rest, will become even more relaxed than it was. As this procedure of creating tension and then releasing it is applied to every major muscle group of the body, all of these muscles will become more relaxed than when you started.

The key to triggering the relaxation response in this manner is to take charge of the voluntary muscles by tensing them and forcing them into a state of relaxation. Once the muscles relax then the other components of the relaxation response will naturally follow. Relaxed muscles require less oxygen so the breathing pattern slows and deepens. The heart does not need to be beating so fast to carry oxygen out to tense muscles. Heart rate and blood pressure decline. The normal blood flow returns to the belly and digestion resumes. The belly is calmed. Hands and feet warm up. Such a series of bodily adaptations all start and fall naturally into place because the voluntary muscles are being directed into a state of relaxation. Soon changes in mood follow, and you become more calm and refreshed.

HOW TO PRACTICALLY DO PROGRESSIVE MUSCLE RELAXATION

To practise progressive muscle relaxation you need to spare a few moments, find a comfortable place, and some amount of privacy. Progressive relaxation can be practised while lying on your back or sitting in a chair with your head supported. Each muscle or muscle group is tensed for 5 seconds, and thereafter, relaxed for 20 seconds. This procedure is repeated at least once. At first only partial relaxation may occur, but after practice the whole body can relax within a few minutes. One has also to **exercise caution** not to tense the neck, back, toes, and feet excessively tight. Tensing these may result in muscle cramping.

1. Sit down or lie down with your eyes closed, feet slightly apart, arms slightly away from sides, and palms upward and make yourself comfortable.
2. Tense all the muscles of your face. Make a tight grimace, keep your eyes closed as tightly as possible, clench your teeth, even move your ears up if you can. Hold this for the count of five as you inhale.
3. Now release your breath slowly and completely. Relax you face muscles. Feel the tension ease away. Enjoy the feel of it.
4. Relax for twenty counts and repeat steps 2 and 3 once again.
5. In this same manner repeating the procedure with the following muscle group:

   Neck and shoulders; chest; abdomen; entire right arm; right forearm and hand (making a fist); right hand; entire left arm; left forearm and hand (again, making a fist); left hand; buttocks; entire right leg; lower right leg and foot; right foot; entire left leg; lower left leg and foot; and the left foot.

AUTOGENIC TRAINING

Autogenic training is a relaxation technique similar to meditation. It is assumed that through a series of self-statements about heaviness and warmth in different parts of the body, a positive effect is induced on the autonomic nervous system. The basic idea of autogenic training is that the body should follow the dictates of the mind. Autogenic training also allows a person to become totally relaxed at any time. Apart from relaxation, autogenic training is believed to influence the organs and the organic system—to quiet the palpitating heart and the nervous stomach. Autogenic training can be helpful in changing unwanted behaviour, because you can use your autogenic skills to work through each of the basic steps of change, by actually feeling the elements of each step with the help of autogenic visualization and suggestion. *Individuals suffering for medical conditions are advised to consult their doctor prior to indulging in this type of relaxation training.*

HOW TO PRACTICALLY DO AUTOGENIC TRAINING

Follow these simple steps one by one. To maintain your proficiency, practise at least once a day. You can achieve a pleasant and calm autogenic state under almost any circumstances.

Find a quiet place free from distractions. Lie on the floor or recline in a chair. Loosen any tight clothing and remove glasses or contacts. Rest your hands in your lap or on the arms of the chair.

1. Take a few slow even breaths. If you have not already, spend a few minutes practising diaphragmatic breathing (the act of breathing deep into your lungs by flexing your diaphragm rather than breathing shallowly by flexing your rib cage). Begin a process of deep breathing, exhaling to a mental count that is twice as long as you inhale. With each breath cycle, increase the duration. For instance, inhale counting, "One," exhale counting, "One, Two." Inhale counting, "One, Two;" exhale counting, "One, Two, Three, Four." Go up the scale to six counts in, twelve counts out. Then reverse: six counts in, twelve counts out; five counts in, ten counts out; and so on, down to one count in, two counts out.
2. Quietly say to yourself, "*I am completely calm.*"
3. Focus attention on your arms. Quietly and slowly, repeat to yourself six times, "*My arms are very heavy.*" Then quietly say to yourself, "*I am completely calm.*"

4. Refocus attention on your arms. Quietly and slowly, repeat to yourself six times, "*My arms are very warm.*" Then quietly say to yourself, "*I am completely calm.*"
5. Focus attention on your legs. Quietly and slowly, repeat to yourself six times, "*My legs are very heavy.*" Then quietly say to yourself, "*I am completely calm.*"
6. Refocus attention on your legs. Quietly and slowly, repeat to yourself six times, "*My legs are very warm.*" Then quietly say to yourself, "*I am completely calm.*"
7. Quietly and slowly, repeat to yourself six times, "*My heartbeat is calm and regular.*" Then quietly say to yourself, "*I am completely calm.*"
8. Quietly and slowly, repeat to yourself six times, "*My breathing is calm and regular.*" Then quietly say to yourself, "*I am completely calm.*"
9. Quietly and slowly, repeat to yourself six times, "*My abdomen is warm.*" Then quietly say to yourself, "*I am completely calm.*"
10. Quietly and slowly, repeat to yourself six times, "*My forehead is pleasantly cool.*" Then quietly say to yourself, "*I am completely calm.*"
11. Enjoy the feeling of relaxation, warmth, and heaviness. When you are ready, quietly say to yourself, "*Arms firm, breathe deeply, eyes open.*"

There are, however, certain cautions to consider. **It is strongly advised** that training take place under the guidance of a qualified instructor. If not properly handled the techniques could be dangerous. Emotional problems could result from improper execution of the techniques. There is also the danger that a person may see autogenic training as a cure-all and neglect needed medical attention.

RELAXATION RESPONSE

The relaxation response represents a form of meditation, which has been practised for many years. The technique can be found in every major religious tradition. It is a simple technique, but it is not easy to practise or to incorporate into your life. You will find your mind wandering, and you will probably find it difficult to set aside the time to practise. It feels like setting aside 20 minutes a day to sit and do nothing.

HOW TO PRACTICALLY DO THE RELAXATION RESPONSE

1. Find a quiet place and sit in a comfortable position. Try to relax your muscles and close your eyes.
2. Concentrate on your breathing. Inhale through your nose and pause for a few seconds. Exhale through your mouth, again pausing for a few seconds.
3. Choose a focus word, phrase, or prayer that has special meaning to you; is firmly rooted in your belief system, or makes you feel peaceful.
4. Repeat that chosen word or phrase or prayer silently to yourself as you exhale.
5. When you notice your mind wandering, as it surely will, just notice it and passively bring your attention back to your breathing.
6. Practise for approximately 20 minutes every day (or at least 3-4 times per week). Do not set an alarm, but sit with a clock in view if necessary.

MEDITATION RELAXATION RESPONSE

The Meditation Relaxation response is a form of meditation. It involves meditating (or focusing the mind) on something in order to create a relaxed response. It is particularly effective at reducing stress, anxiety, depression, and other negative emotions. There are varieties of techniques and it is very important that we chose the right one for which we are mentally equipped. It is thus best to begin by choosing the simple techniques, which enable in minimizing change of external diversion and maximizing the focus on one single object. Three such basic techniques are being outlined here, which will be useful for beginners.

COUNT YOUR BREATH MEDITATION

This is simply a meditation to focus on the rhythm of your breath by counting your in and out breath. It is very easy to do, and at first, you mind will start wandering around. Do not worry about it, as it is quite natural. Just gently acknowledge that and shift your mind back into counting your breath again. With time, your mind will slow down and will stop wandering by itself, without any external 'nudging'. To practise this type of meditation follow the steps outlined:

1. Sit down, close your eyes, and concentrate on your breathing. Be aware of every breathing in and breathing out.
2. Do not try to control your breathing, or try to slow it down forcefully. Just breath automatically, freely and pay attention to the air passing through your nose, lungs and goes out again.
3. After a few breaths, start counting.
4. Breathing in, one…breathing out, two……breathing in, three……breathing out, four… breathing in, five… breathing out, six
5. Should you find yourself thinking of something else instead of your breathing, just acknowledge it, return to your breathing, and start counting again
6. Now, notice the sensations of your breathing. The depth, the speed, see if your breathing becomes increasingly slower and quieter, if your breathing more and more goes to your stomach or your chest, if your body becomes more relaxed through your breathing, …etc. Try to notice this as an outsider, without stopping from counting. If you cannot, then just go back to counting
7. Breathing in, breathing out, breathing in, breathing out, etc.
8. If at any time you notice any strange feelings in your body, like twinkling, or muscle reactions, just notice that, it is quite normal. Go back to your breathing
9. Once you got to hundred, slowly return to normal, open your eyes, take in everything you see in the room, get up from the chair, and stretch your muscles
10. You are done!

FLAME MEDITATION

There are different techniques that are commonly used, but it would be appropriate to start any of them by relaxing your body, mind and emotions in whatever way you have found that lets this happen. Position yourself in a way that will allow you to remain alert, comfortable, and undistracted. The place you are in should be conducive to meditation. Often this will include a room that is quiet except for pleasant music playing in the background, has fragrant aromas from incense or flowers, and beautiful furnishings and decorations. Place a lit candle on the floor about 3 to 6 feet in front of you—where your gaze falls naturally downward, or on a table in front of you that places the flame of the candle at about eye level. Turn off the lights, making sure that you still have some light entering the room, so you have the room in semi-dark. Being as empty as possible, simply gaze at the flame. Silently focus on the flame. Try not to think of the flame or the candle. Every time you wander away in your thoughts return to the candle-flame without judging. Your inner chatterer will probably comment, compare, and judge. Let it do its thing and the chatter will eventually slow and possibly even stop. Just watch the flame's soothing dance. Follow the procedure systematically outlined ahead. This exercise will help train the mind and third eye to direct psychic energy.

1. Put your candle at a place where you can see it well.
2. Sit down, close your eyes, and concentrate on your breathing.
3. Be aware of each breath taken in and exhaled out.
4. Breathe automatically and freely, do not try to control your breathing.
5. Pay attention to how the air slowly passes through your nose, fills up your lungs, and goes out again.
6. If, after taking a few breaths, you feel fine and at ease, you open your eyes and focus all your attention to the flame.
7. Breathe deeply and steadily and stare at the flame. Try not to think of the candle, the flame, this exercise, or other matters. When you start to think of something else than the flame, just return to the flame.
8. Breathe deeply and steadily and stare at the flame.

9. If all of a sudden you notice twinkling in your body or relaxation reactions in your muscles, that is all right.....just observe and return to your object.
10. Continue doing this during the period of time you had set apart for this exercise.
11. If you like, you can now close your eyes and try to see the flame at the inside of your eyelids.
12. With your mind's eye look at and visualize the flame as long as you can.
13. When the image disappears or you start thinking of other things, just try to get the image of the flame projected in front of your eyes again.
14. Do this as long as you like or for the duration of the period, you had in mind.
15. All right, now slowly take your thoughts back to the rest of your body and the sounds in the room. Move a little, stretch your muscles a little, and open your eyes.
16. It is now finished and you will feel relaxed.

RELAXATION USING VISUALIZATION

One of the simplest relaxation techniques is the use of visualization. Visualization, or *guided imagery*, is a variation on traditional meditation that can help relieve stress. When used as a relaxation technique, guided imagery involves imagining a scene in which you feel at peace, free to let go of all tension and anxiety. Choose whatever setting is most calming to you, whether a tropical beach, a favourite childhood spot, or a quiet wooded glen. You can do this visualization exercise on your own, with a therapist's help, or using an audio recording. Follow these simple steps and see the wonder they create.

1. Close your eyes.
2. Let your worries drift away.
3. Imagine your restful place.
4. Picture it as vividly as you can—everything you can see, hear, smell, and feel.
5. Gently banish disruptive thoughts. Use your imagination to help to shoo away the intrusive thoughts that love to pop

up, particularly when we are trying to enjoy some peace and quiet. Attach the thought to a colourful bird flying in the sky or the sun rising from behind the snow-clad mountains.

6. Enjoy. This is your time to be quiet and relaxed so that you can recharge your batteries. Keep telling yourself that this is your special place, where you are completely safe, and where all of your worries and concerns are far away.

Guided imagery works best if you incorporate as many sensory details as possible. If you are thinking about a dock on a quiet lake:

- **See** the sun setting over the water.
- **Hear** the birds singing.
- **Smell** the pine trees.
- **Feel** the cool water on your bare feet.
- **Taste** the fresh, clean air.

GETTING THE MOST OUT OF YOUR RELAXATION PRACTICE

Set aside time in your daily schedule

The best way to start and maintain a relaxation practice is by incorporating it into your daily routine. Schedule a set time either once or twice a day for your practice. You may find that it is easier to stick with your practice if you do it first thing in the morning, before other tasks and responsibilities get in the way.

Do not practice when you are sleepy

These techniques can relax you so much that they can make you very sleepy, especially if it is close to bedtime. You will get the most out of these techniques if you practise when you are fully awake and alert.

Choose a technique that appeals to you

There is no single relaxation technique best suitable for all. When choosing a relaxation technique, consider your specific needs, preferences, and fitness level. The right relaxation technique is the one that resonates with you and fits your lifestyle.

Any thing that encourages the body to become more relaxed may be used as relaxation therapy. Some more easy relaxation techniques include a relaxing bath, relaxing music, body massage, practising yoga, aerobics, or even a plain simple stretch out on a chair or bed without thinking about anything. However, in many instances, a relaxation technique, which reduces stress and anxiety for one individual, may actually be a stressful situation that aggravates anxiety for another individual. It thus becomes important that individuals should find for themselves the stress reduction, relaxation techniques that actually work for them. It is very important to note that the same relaxation technique may not work for every individual because of individual differences in personality make up as well as differences in situation and circumstances.

Chapter 23

Living With The Devils – How To Remain Mentally Healthy

"People who are emotionally healthy are in control of their emotions and their behaviour. They are able to handle life's inevitable challenges, build strong relationships, and lead productive, fulfilling lives. When bad things happen, they are able to bounce back and move on... In order to maintain and strengthen your mental and emotional health, it is important to pay attention to your own needs and feelings. Do not let stress and negative emotions build up. Try to maintain a balance between your daily responsibilities and the things you enjoy. If you take care of yourself, you will be better prepared to deal with challenges if and when they arise".

"Mental health is a condition and level of social functioning which is socially acceptable and personally satisfying"

If you want to develop into a healthy individual, it is very important to have a good mental health. You need to be in as a psychological state of well-being, characterized by continuing personal growth, a sense of purpose in life, self-acceptance, and positive relations with others. You mental health is dependent upon your attitudes towards life and the psychological, environmental, genetic, or physiological factors that have a profound effect on your overall mental development. How well you cope and adjust with life is the determining factor of your mental health.

SOME FACTORS INFLUENCING MENTAL HEALTH – A QUICK REVIEW

One's mental health has a huge impact on every aspect of life. A person with a good mental health is always appreciative of achievements and readily accepts his shortcomings. On the other hand, if one does not have a good mental health it can lead to feelings of inferiority. Such a person devalues his own self, forming a negative image of his body. He can harbour intense feelings of self-hate, anger, disgust, and uselessness. Such feelings can transform into extreme depression, psychosocial disorders, or eating disorders – many of which we will discuss further in the series.

Mental health also effects education. Good mental health assures an all-round educational experience that enhances social and intellectual skills leading to self-confidence and better grades. People who lack good mental health generally tend to isolate themselves developing anxiety disorders and concentration problems.

Relationships are also affected by one's mental health because the functioning of relationships is based on it. If one is not mentally healthy, his interactions with family, friends, and colleagues may not be positively oriented. They will find it difficult to nurture relationships and face problems with commitment or intimacy, frequently also encountering sexual health issues.

People with good mental health have a good sleep during the night. This is so because they are generally devoid of stress and anxiety. A mentally healthy individual can effectively cope with stress and anxiety. A bad mental health can lead to sleep disturbances causing insomnia. This, in turn, leaves one exhausted, and reduces efficiency levels.

The effect of mental health can also be directly seen on physical health. Stress generally can lead to hypertension and this in turn can lead to many other disorders.

HOW TO BE MENTALLY HEALTHY

Mental health is the adjustment of human beings to the world and to each other with a maximum of effectiveness and happiness. It is not just efficiency, or just contentment—or the grace of obeying the rules of the game cheerfully. It is all of these together. It is the ability to maintain an even temper, an alert intelligence, socially considerate behaviour, and a happy disposition – this is what a healthy mind is.

Throughout this book, I have mentioned and highlighted the various ways in which one can remain mentally healthy. It is important that we make a conscious effort to improve and maintain our mental health. Here are some points, which will help you in achieving a good mental health. Following the tips given, will assure you of a mentally healthy life. Remember you have to keep following the advice given on a day-to-day basis until it becomes a healthy habit.

1. **Develop within you adequate feelings of security**. Identify the insecurities within and around you. Some may be real and most of them imaginary. Work out solutions for the real ones and forget the unreal ones. Insecurities generally arise due to lack of faith in us. We feel inadequate in handling the difficult situations in life. We begin to worry about our future. We give up our struggles and quit. Do not quit. Handle the present and future will take care of itself.

2. **Do honest and adequate self-evaluation**. Know yourself. Identify your strengths and accept your weaknesses. Accepting your weaknesses will strengthen you. Overcome your weaknesses and make them your strength. You will have a stronger arsenal.
3. **Develop adequate spontaneity and emotionality**. You should be spontaneous in all your doings. Do not wait for a push or pull. Charge your energies and remain fully charged. Be emotionally warm to others because what you give you receive. Receiving emotional warmth from others is good for your mental health.
4. **Maintain efficient contact with reality**. Diana Hayden quoted in the miss universe pageant "In dreams begin realities". Even if you are a dreamer then let your dreams be positively oriented so that you can turn them into realities. Learn to live in this world and not outside it.
5. **Have adequate bodily desires and the ability to gratify them**. Man surely cannot live by bread alone. He needs to fulfil his other biological needs as well and have the ability to do so. Eat, drink, sleep, and be merry. You should eat adequately and sleep adequately. However, not every one of us gets to fulfil these desires at the same price. Many have to pay heavily for adequate food and sleep. If you are one of them then work out your schedule so that you can afford this luxury. It will surely benefit you. A healthy mind in a healthy body is a very old saying.
6. **Have adequate self-knowledge**. Know thyself and health will follow. Many of us are ignorant about ourselves. We tend to either underestimate or overestimate ourselves. Both have their disadvantages. We are what we are and not what we think we are. However, we should always think positive about ourselves because if we do not have the good we think we have we can have it. Go get it.
7. **Have an integrated and consistent personality**. We have to put ourselves together. We have to have consistency in thought and action. Avoid having a split personality. Remember united you stand and divided you fall. The same applies for

personality. A well-integrated and consistent individual will be strong and always mentally healthy.

8. **Have adequate life goals**. A life without motive is virtually a life without a purpose. You are in this world with some purpose. Define your aims and objectives in life. Set your goals and go out to achieve them. See the pleasure that achievement brings. It gives you happiness and joy that is the key to a good mental health.
9. **Learn from experiences**. A burnt child dreads the fire but as he grows, he also learns the positive utilities of fire. We all have good as well as bad experiences in life. We learn from both. Bad experiences teach us how to constantly have good ones. Surely, there is no better a teacher in this world than experience.
10. **Develop the ability to satisfy the requirements of the group**. Man is a social animal who is constantly in active interaction with other individuals. We give and we receive. We have to go along with the norms of society. We have to satisfy the social requirements and norms. We have to resonate in consonance to avoid dissonance.

MAINTAINING GOOD MENTAL HEALTH

The ability to cope with adversity can be crucial for the mental health of the individual. *Coping* means successfully dealing with problems that arise in life. People differ substantially in the way they cope with adversity. Some people engage in *emotion-focused coping,* a strategy that focuses on managing one's emotions. Examples of this coping strategy include distracting one's attention from the problem, denying the problem, venting one's emotions, or sharing emotions with others. A second form of coping, *problem-focused coping*, involves efforts to reduce stress by solving the problem. People who use this strategy take active steps to overcome the problem, such as seeing a counsellor to repair a relationship or looking for a new job in response to problems at work. They may also seek advice from friends and family members.

Some people use coping skills more effectively than others do. However, research has shown that people can learn new coping skills.

For example, counsellors can teach children how to handle difficulties in school. Adults can be taught skills to cope with stressful life events, such as job loss and divorce. Teaching people coping skills before they encounter adversity, or early in the stages of a crisis, appears an effective method of preventing poor mental health. Learning effective coping strategies also directly improves mental health by improving one's sense of mastery and self-esteem.

Social support from friends and family members also promotes good mental health. This support can take several forms. Other people can offer concrete help in a crisis, such as providing shelter to families victimized by a natural disaster or alerting an unemployed person to a job opportunity. In addition, other people can provide an important source of emotional support. Friends respond with concern, empathy, and advice to a person facing difficulties or loss. They boost confidence and self-esteem by offering reassurance and compliments. Self-help groups provide support by enabling people with similar problems to share their experiences and emotions. Conversely, research has shown that negative social interactions, such as constant criticism and belittlement from other people, can undermine mental health.

Other ways of maintaining good mental health involve physical activities. For example, research has shown that regular aerobic exercise helps to boost self-esteem, relieve depression, and improve concentration. Relaxation techniques, such as deep breathing and meditation, also help to combat the effects of stress.

I wish you a good mental health hoping that you will follow the advice, you have read in this book, on a regular basis. If in case you have any queries then you can write to me at samvaidna@hotmail.com and share your problems with me. I will be glad to help you tame the little devils within you. You can also join the Page - Samvaidna: The Mental Health Organization on Face Book where your problem will be addressed by a group of professionally trained clinical psychologists and counsellors on its discussion page.